VONNEGUT

Kennikat Press
National University Publications
Literary Criticism Series

General Editor
John E. Becker
Fairleigh Dickinson University

RICHARD GIANNONE

VONNEGUT

A PREFACE
TO HIS NOVELS

National University Publications
KENNIKAT PRESS   //   1977
Port Washington, N. Y.   //   London

813.54
Gi √

Manufactured in the United States of America

Published by
Kennikat Press Corp.
Port Washington, N. Y./London

Library of Congress Cataloging in Publication Data

Giannone, Richard.
    Vonnegut: a preface to his novels.

    (Literary criticism series) (National university publications)
    Bibliography: p.
    Includes index.
    1. Vonnegut, Kurt—Criticism and interpretation.
PS3572.05Z68   813'.5'4   76-54943
ISBN 0-8046-9167-3

For Martin Geller and Wendy Gimbel

CONTENTS

FOREWORD

By using the word *Preface* in the subtitle of this book, I want to suggest not only its introductory character but also the method and movement by which the discussion leads the reader through Kurt Vonnegut's novels. Leaving aside his short stories, my plan is to put before the reader a systematic inquiry into the features of Vonnegut's novelistic art as it develops. To this end, the major topics of each novel are explored at some length because to consider the themes is to track the range of Vonnegut's talent. Each chapter surveys thematic affinities among the novels before taking up the texts singly to show how Vonnegut's recurring subjects are realized in particular fictions. The analysis pays special attention to the ways in which the issues that preoccupy the novelist give a work its distinctive design. Among all the aspects of Vonnegut's imagination, it is form that is most frequently slighted; and yet it is the forms of his novels which offer evidence of his accomplishment.

Vonnegut's subject is no single, static thing, of course. Since the publication in 1952 of his first novel, his interests undergo considerable expansion; his manner accordingly acquires an experimental energy that endows the shapes of his novels with increasing complexity. This evolution of Vonnegut's artistry is the story of his mind behind the fictive stories that he tells. Once the overarching changes have been traced, the reader can approach the novels with a sense of the coherence of Vonnegut's thought. While considering individual meaning and pattern in a book, then, the analytical treatment looks forward to how that novel emerges from a continuing moral concern and yet marks a departure from what was said in preceding books. And because his total effort derives further significance from the genre he works in, this study takes into account how Vonnegut's experimentation stands over against our customary expectation about how a novel is put together.

Again, calling this book a *Preface* implies that each reader will make independent discoveries in the artistic text, and this preface to Vonnegut's novels will fulfill its purpose if readers make anew for themselves the observations offered. To catalyze such interaction with the text, I have pursued certain reflections through which the reader might enter with excitement the urgent comments made by the novels on how we live now. Here I hope to bring into play the artist's passionate inner struggle to penetrate the mystery of life underlying the dread and emptiness that are so comprehensively rendered in his dramatic action. Writing is, at root, a contemplative act for Vonnegut, and we need to be introduced to this presupposition to perceive his affirming warmth within his spare and vivid and iconoclastic prose. During a Congressional symposium on the legal rights of authors held in Washington on June 18, 1975, he alerted us to this, his strongest conviction, when he said that "writing . . . requires a sustained, profound meditation." Fiction conceived as meditation finds its full meaning, not in any surface of the text, but in a movement of the spirit, which requires the reader to relate to the inner force of the words. Only an equally sustained and collaborative act of generous attentiveness on the reader's part can touch the artist's composing deep.

I have received support for my work, and I want to acknowledge Fordham University for awarding me a faculty fellowship and Union Theological Seminary for extending its gracious hospitality during my fruitful year as Visiting Scholar.

Finally, a personal word. One does not have to read far into Vonnegut's writing to notice the high value he places on friendship. The motif of mutual esteem rises in each of his novels. "What is life without friends?" asks the lonely, confessing narrator of *Mother Night*. Amid the terror and falsity that make up the human condition in Vonnegut's world, friends can momentarily liberate each other by listening to the neglected voice from their concealed inner depth. Friends make life possible. In the course of writing this book I have enjoyed the affection that Vonnegut has written about. I thank Joseph Chaikin, William Coco, Anne Geller, Bernard Steinzor, and Jean-Claude van Itallie for their gifts of spirit.

Richard Giannone

INTRODUCTION

> I ate my food between massacres.
> The shadow of murder lay upon my sleep.
> Bertolt Brecht, *To Posterity*

The striking name Vonnegut derives from a stream in Germany called the Vonne; and though the life story of its famous bearer Kurt Vonnegut— who has made his name even more curious by retaining the "Jr." until the recent publication of *Slapstick*—returns to its German origin in a crucial way, his history flows from Indianapolis, Indiana, where he grew up in a typically middle-American way. His maternal grandfather owned a brewery that won a Gold Medal at the Paris Exposition for its Lieber Lager (coffee was its secret ingredient). His paternal side was artistic. Both his grandfather and father were respected local architects.

Edith Lieber and Kurt Vonnegut senior had three children. The oldest, Bernard, now a noted physicist, was born in 1914; a daughter Alice, a sculptor, was born in 1917 and died in 1957, at which time three of her four sons became part of the novelist's family, making six children in all. On Armistice Day, November 11, 1922, the now-celebrated Kurt Vonnegut, Jr., was born. Armistice Day has become Veterans' Day; and the coincidence of Vonnegut's birth on a day commemorating those seasoned by military experience and the cessation of hostilities foreshadowed a great deal about what was to be central in his life.

The story of America since Vonnegut's birth is a story of catastrophes: the boom-to-bust 1920s; the great depression; World War II; the postwar dawning of the atomic age; the Korean War; the crimes of Vietnam; the flurry of assassinations; the era of Nixonian duplicity. For most Americans misfortune is to be gotten through and forgotten in the pursuit of happiness. Vonnegut, however, reflected on the disasters that shaped his life, and he developed a mind practiced at examining their larger implications. As he questioned, he found a history patterned by greed and senseless destruction that had reached the point of threatening humanity with extinction. Vonnegut's brooding made him very much a veteran of our recent past; and his energy has gone into making peace, establishing an armistice, with the adversities that he found molding human destiny. For Vonnegut, crisis became a way of looking at the moment.

He was a child of the depression. While sharing in the very real adversity and tragedy suffered by millions of Americans, he felt the need to work against what he later called the era's "life-hating mood"[1] that made joy undesirable and gratification impossible. At the time, dignity was narrowly based on material security. After graduating from Shortridge High School in 1940, Vonnegut went to Cornell University to study biochemistry. His father, who had not held a job for ten years during the depression, felt that science would assure his son a job. The essential poverty of the depression, Vonnegut came to learn, was spiritual. People were made to feel useless; their hardship was to generate a self out of their feelings of inadequacy. This mood of inner deprivation pervades Vonnegut's writing and underlies his concept of the self.

If the 1930s gave him this ethos, Indiana, where Vonnegut learned about human loss, provided him with a cultural setting in which to write about it. When not actually set in Indiana, the locale of his tales is never very far emotionally from home, for the Hoosier State becomes Vonnegut's *patria* in the way that Ohio does for Anderson and Nebraska for Cather—the province by which the world at large is measured. The American heartland for Vonnegut is a ruin. Usually, the situation in his fiction is that of despair—statistically average citizens living out the programmed lives of their conditioned, modest ambition. Our nationally treasured ordinariness disguises desperation, violence, and philistinism. If there are occasional moments of simple tenderness in day-to-day encounters, there is also an astonishing amount of unexamined cruelty. Vonnegut's method of exploring such a common life ranges from the amusingly quizzical to the condemnatory; but when the sensitive inner surface of its pain is laid bare, a homey compassion lifts that sorrow into dignity by revealing the deeply human quality in our ordinariness. Vonnegut's underlying sympathy seems to arise from the very class he criticizes. In fact, apart from his exalting the imagination, Vonnegut's values are those we associate with middle-class virtues. Decency, respect, neighborliness, success, and security are what his characters look for; and in the end, that commonplace search is rendered so tenderly that we can say that middle America also gave Vonnegut a moral scale.

At Cornell, though he studied chemistry, Vonnegut also responded to his own inner needs by writing a great deal. He wrote for the *Cornell Daily Sun,* which, then as now, was a commercial operation; so his professional identity as a writer came early. In his junior year of college, which he began at Carnegie Tech, he forsook his publicly avowed opposition to World War II, which America had just entered, and joined the American army as an infantry private. (The surprise bombing of Pearl Harbor changed the minds of many who opposed U. S. intervention.) While on patrol as a battalion scout in Germany, he was taken prisoner and sent to Dresden to work at a factory that made malt syrup for pregnant women.

On February 13, 1945, during the time Vonnegut was a prisoner, the Allied air forces, led by the R. A. F., attacked Dresden; and the bombardment reached into Vonnegut's soul. He has told the story of his surviving the holocaust many times—most passionately in *Slaughterhouse-Five* (1969). Two features of the event always stand out in his telling. There was the sheer grotesque technological wizardry that rapidly annihilated 135,000 human beings in two hours as waves of planes first dropped bombs to gut the buildings, then poured down incendiary bombs, which were followed by more high explosives. Eventually the whole of Dresden would, in his own words, "join up into one apocalyptic flame with tornadoes around the edges sucking more and more, feeding the inferno."[2] All of this to a great, defenseless cultural city that had been declared open and had no military value. In Vonnegut's memory Dresden loomed as the end of the world with its grim judgment of human malice. But beyond the question of the savage cruelty of the Allied fire-bombing, there was for Vonnegut the question of moral response. American newspapers carried nothing about Dresden. To Vonnegut the absence of horror was itself a horrible indictment of our moral sense that made him feel responsible in conscience to say something. And he knew then that people were capable, probably eager, to wipe out life on earth. Dresden deepened Vonnegut's dark habit of mind into starkness by leaving a memory through which he interpreted human history and pondered our future.

He came home in 1945, returned to Cornell briefly, then went to the University of Chicago to study anthropology for three years. (In Chicago he also worked as a reporter.) Vonnegut has had a long history of involvement and irritation with the academic scene. He has been a student, faculty member (Iowa, Harvard, City College), guest speaker (Bennington, Wheaton, Brown), swami, and subject of doctoral dissertations; but he has found the university atmosphere as arid and mechanized intellectually as the rest of society is politically. After the University of Chicago, he lived in Schenectady and worked at General Electric, writing publicity for the Research Laboratory, at which his brother Bernard had been working on nucleation of supercooled liquids. Public relations work brought Vonnegut close to one of the centers of technology responsible for the dreary sameness of American life that he had always decried. Profit motives, he saw, were couched in sentimental tributes to pure science; individual freedom was sacrificed for professional advancement; and research was conducted without regard for its necessity or desirability. He saw that technology was developed in a moral vacuum. Like the Midwest, Schenectady gave him a place and perspective for his fiction. He renamed it Ilium, New York, in the novels to call attention to the distance between the heroic aspiration of ancient Troy and the shabbiness of its modern counterpart. Vonnegut's pun draws on the spirit of Greek revival that gave upstate New York its numerous classical names, such as Ithaca, Syracuse, Attica, Rome. Vonnegut's Ilium stands not as a patrician monument to the grand American dream, but rather, as a reminder of the need for a genuine rebirth of culture and feeling in American life. Unlike his view from Indiana, the attitude toward Ilium is uniformly negative, ranging from ridicule to bitterness. While grinding out platitudes about the wonder of electricity at General Electric, he was writing his own stories, just as he kept trust with his talent at Cornell by writing while studying science. He sold his stories to *Collier's* and *The Saturday Evening Post*.

In 1950 he quit General Electric and went to Barnstable on the north shore of Cape Cod to devote himself to his writing. Always the pro, he wanted to write for a livelihood; and he needed to make money to support his large family. His decision to be a professional writer proved economically feasible, though it was rough going artistically. Vonnegut had to do a great deal of free-lance hack work for science-fiction magazines such as *Galaxy* and *Fantasy,* which paid well enough to keep him afloat. When he was serious, that work met with misunderstanding. As a rule, misjudgment is not surprising for innovative writers; and as for Vonnegut, who had an active commercial reputation to color the reaction to his work, a misreading of his deeper intention is expected. His first novel, *Player Piano*

(1952), was called *Utopia 14* for one edition and salaciously packaged as a drugstore quick-sale. *The Sirens of Titan* (1959) and *Mother Night* (1962) were victims of the same promotion. We would do well, however, not to interpret Vonnegut's publishing history in light of his present wealthy eminence with its special prerogatives, and to resist the urge to turn his publishers into villains and his motives into artistic compromises. Vonnegut needed money, which he earned by writing. Hardcover publication came about with *Cat's Cradle* (1963) and *God Bless You, Mr. Rosewater* (1965). Still, Vonnegut's career had two directions—there was his success as a writer for popular magazines and there was his serious work that was critically unrecognized and confined to a very limited readership.

His career changed in 1969 when Seymour Lawrence, an independent Boston publisher, brought out *Slaughterhouse-Five.* Everything came together: he wrote about the unstoried massacre of Dresden, which had been on his mind, at the same time that he used his experience as a science fictionist to show how technology was promoting disasters. *Slaughterhouse-Five* was a personal victory that became a public triumph. Critical admiration for his Dresden book brought about an interest in his earlier work which has catalyzed close consideration of his art.

Great success, such as that which *Slaughterhouse-Five* bestowed on Vonnegut, can prompt a writer to rethink his artistic aims. Vonnegut did just that. Then, feeling that he had turned a corner in his work, he decided to write plays. He wrote *Happy Birthday, Wanda June,* which opened in New York in 1970, and then wrote a special for public television in 1972 called *Between Time and Timbuktu.* Dissatisfied with the theater, he quit the stage and allowed the novel that he had finished but withheld from publication to appear. *Breakfast of Champions* came out in 1973 and marked Vonnegut's return to print. Richer and happier now, he assures us, Vonnegut has achieved that stature at which "absolutely anything I write is going to sell extremely well . . . it's going to sell phenomenally."[3]

Automatic popularity can be an artistic trap for a writer because it encourages repetition of the old applauded forms, which is the death of art. Vonnegut's recent collection of opinions, *Wampeters, Foma & Granfalloons* (1974), however, reveals precisely the self-criticism required to work against his own successful formulations. Here we see Vonnegut in his shirtsleeves examining his personal values in relation to topical issues in order to grow emotionally. There are reviews, addresses, essays, and interviews from 1965 to 1973 which are the workings of an open, generous intelligence putting itself on the line. The book has the ring of testimony modulated through the intimate musings of a confession. Pacificism and social convictions are out front. A Nixon is called a Nixon; and our national conscience is challenged when he takes up some of the world's neglected miseries, such as Biafra and the American Indians, that we have become hardened to. The collection amounts to a call, especially to its author, for emotional and political reform. These pieces, moreover, tell us that writing for Vonnegut carries with it the moral power of committing himself to himself by answering his "inner urgency,"[4] as he puts it, to be the subject of his own work, and making himself the subject of his writing is precisely what he does in *Slapstick* (1976).

In a 1975 issue of the *New York Times Book Review*, Vonnegut reviewed Tom Wicker's *A Time to Die*, which treats of the September 1971 uprising at the Attica State Correctional Facility. What took place was, in the words of the State Special Commission on Attica, "the bloodiest one-day encounter between Americans in this century." Beyond Vonnegut's stated admiration for Wicker's reporting the atrocity with the same daring he showed as mediator, we can see in the review an uncanny link to Vonnegut's own sensibility and work, a correspondence that remains unstated but noteworthy. The upstate Attica uprising in 1971 actualizes the imagined rebellion that Vonnegut dramatizes in his upstate New York novel, *Player Piano*, published nineteen years earlier. The rage in both the fictive and real insurgence is that of the disenfranchised against an unjust, dehumanizing system. Vonnegut finds the Wicker book significant, and the telling appeal is Wicker's genius in transforming an objective report into "a melancholy biography."[5] What Vonnegut esteems in Wicker's journalism is what we will come to see as the creative energy in Vonnegut's fictions, for such interpenetration between life and art brings about his rich experimentation with novelistic forms. In his nonfiction prose Vonnegut found the world as irrational and genocidal as he depicted it in his narratives; and his artistic forms, to cite Theodore Roethke, whom he respects, propose "to maintain self against the disruptive whole."[6] Vonnegut pieces himself together by composing a melancholy biography of his own, out of which he manages as well to make some marvelous jokes, revealing the exuberant side of his nature.

II

Vonnegut's jokes have the peculiar quality of grimness that surrounds the dark laughter of our age. There is a technical psychoanalytic word, hebephrenia, to describe that extreme psychic habit which alters one's inner feeling to express its opposite; and the condition marks the sensibility to which Vonnegut is keenly attuned. In one of his interviews he recalls that his "peak funniness" was achieved in a time of horror and shock. He was appearing at a literary festival given by the University of Notre Dame in April, 1968. The audience was so keyed up that everything he did or said came off as hilarious. Though the auditorium was huge, a mere cough or the clearing of his throat broke up the whole place. A political tragedy had occurred, and the public terror had invaded the room to sensitize the audience to this nervous mirth. "People were laughing because they were in agony, full of pain they couldn't do anything about. They said sick and helpless because Martin Luther King had been shot two days before."[7] Laughing in the presence of grief not only bespeaks a psychic displacement but also defines well that gallows humor which has swept over contemporary American writing with sufficient force to require identification. We call it black humor. Such comic posturing conveys the disquieting conviction that things are so bad that we must laugh at them or be engulfed. This mimicry of fun when in despondency is unique because it seems the only available means of dealing with experience that continually brings pain. Vonnegut's narrative jokes before misery have so poignantly spoken to the hebephrenic tone of our mind that he has become a cult hero.

Despite the adulation and the enormous popularity of his fiction, Vonnegut's art remains a puzzlement—puzzling both in its material and its idiom. The kind of connections through motivation and causality that we are trained to make are discouraged. His novels call attention to their novelty: heroes vanish; narrative time goes out of kilter; worlds exist within worlds; beginning interchanges with ending; realistic action is denied; a story line is overtaken by a digression. What the reader encounters is an attempt to build a fictive structure out of seemingly random events experienced by phantom creatures. Moreover, our instinctive effort to get at the principles organizing the array is made harder by a self-mocking tone that tells us to disregard its complication.

Critics, trying to catch up with Vonnegut's readership, have tried to explain his complex art by variously labeling him black humorist, science fiction writer, space fantasist, absurdist, visionary, prophet. All are true but partial. These rivaling critical interests do serve to alert us to the serious side of his playful tales. In fact, his novels are comic masks covering the tragic farce that is our contemporary life; and for all his technical experimentation, his subject is the enduring humanistic trust that he averred when he said, in his 1970 address at Bennington College, that "humanity is at the center of the universe, the fulfiller or the frustrator of the grandest dreams of God Almighty."[8]

The public statement of his belief is misleadingly final and simple because in the fiction we find that the opposite obtains. Humans feel eccentric in the universe; and when they do find a place, their success is a qualified victory replete with failure. The grand story of Vonnegut's novels, considered collectively, is the working out of this faith. As we might expect, he proceeds circuitously, for the art of Kurt Vonnegut is like a web. At the center of the design are the questions: What is it to be human? What is the purpose of life? Why is there so much suffering? How can suffering be borne? Radiating from this center are the conditions Vonnegut believes deprive us of our sense of what makes humans human. The thematic filaments binding the web are the dehumanizing effects of modern technocracy, the psychic damage experienced by individuals when the spiritual stuffing is knocked out of them, the religious lies we substitute for mutual trust, the cultural refuse filling our emptiness, greed, war, our self-destruction, and finally, the struggle of the imagination to deal with the moral ruin within and around us.

There are many interconnecting themes. Some we have come to expect of any writer who thinks deeply about our time: homelessness, violence, political corruption, exploitation, massacre. Other issues, such as sabotage, make-believe, prophecy, space trips, crusading, simple-mindedness, and the virtue of imperfection are peculiarly Vonnegut. These themes come together in various ways. Vonnegut sometimes treats his story directly; other times he handles grave matters playfully and light things solemnly. He is by turns traditional and experimental in recounting his tale. And then, as he grows confident, he takes liberties, scattering graffiti, memos, word catalogues, playlets, and drawings about his books. So Vonnegut's art is a complicated web.

The important point for now is not the wonderful intricacy of the pattern (that is for later), but its basic unity. We need to see that Vonnegut's work is of a piece. He did not suddenly become serious after putting in time as a magazine hack. Nor did his critically acclaimed later fiction come out of a hat. From the beginning of his career, Vonnegut was dealing with the critical issues that we identify with his 1969 novel, *Slaughterhouse-Five,* for example. If we approach his work canonically with an eye for wholeness, we will be in a position to discriminate. Passing interests will be seen as such; the books will clarify one another; and we will see what is essential by observing how it takes hold in subsequent works. Above all, we will be able to identify the new shapes his themes assume, the formal changes which define Vonnegut's growth as an artist. Again, a sense of the wholeness of Vonnegut's work is important here. Some writers—Keats and Faulkner, for example—grow by a radical shift in thought. The minds of others mature by deepening, by becoming more of what they initially are. This, we will see, is Vonnegut's way.

1

PLAYER PIANO

> Let your life be a counter friction to the machine.
>
> Thoreau, *Civil Disobedience*

Vonnegut's first novel, *Player Piano,* was published in 1952. The title refers to an antique musical instrument found in a saloon frequented by many of the characters in the story. It symbolizes the individual's passive relation to an American society in its advanced technological stage: the human person is a phantom, an idle musician, seated at an electronically bobbing keyboard that clangs out a prepunched tune which the player is not actually playing. Reduced to an extension of a device that is its own cause and effect, the player is dispensable. The piano's sounds, moreover, are brassy and ghoulish and inhuman mockeries of the emotion music appeals to.

This musical relic is an amusing version of a greater and more sinister instrument in the novel that manipulates an entire society. The device is a computer imposingly named EPICAC XIV to dramatize its advanced development. EPICAC XIV has the capacity to create a total political and social system according to its abstract specifications. When the novel was reissued in 1954 by a paperback house, it was fittingly retitled *Utopia 14* to evoke the mechanized paradise born of EPICAC XIV. The perfection of this utopia derives from the precise decisions of computer logic. Nothing is too trivial for its plan, since it even decides how many pinochle decks are to be produced in a given year. Nothing is too complex, for the computer establishes what I. Q. levels are useless, or useless at a given time. It also provides grades of truth. EPICAC XIV is electromagnetics as morality, fate, and ontology. Vonnegut is considering the dire warning issued by Norbert Wiener in his seminal treatise on the social implications of the computer, *The Human Use of Human Beings,* that technological expertise unaccompanied by a clear understanding of human purpose endangers society. It seems likely, too, that Vonnegut took his image of the player piano from Wiener, who illustrates his distinction between "know-how" and "know-what" with a vignette of a prominent American engineer who buys an expensive player piano to satisfy his interest in the piano mechanism but has no sense of the instrument's means of producing music.[1] Vonnegut, however, makes more ominous use of Wiener's tale of the player piano, for the novel shows a society that gradually surrenders its humanity to artificial intelligence through an inhuman use of human beings.

For all the ultramodernity of its theme, cybernetics, the book is markedly conventional. It is, I would say, Vonnegut's least experimental and least interesting novel. He leaves aside the futuristic aspects of his subject in favor of showing the human side, depicting in a straightforward manner how people live at a time when their "know-how" has outrun their "know-what." The action takes up the process of human defilement by machines at midpoint—that is, when the process is well under way but has by no means reached the ultimate mechanized state of the projected Utopia 14.

In the America of *Player Piano,* the life of each citizen is abbreviated to an electronically sensitive personnel card for the computer to arrange into its vast scheme. Unlike Wiener's vision of a machine serving humans by replacing human functions that have been impaired, this machine impairs people themselves. The built-in purpose of the system efficiency subordinates individuals to its organism. The result in the moral atmosphere is a ruling sense of uselessness that is subtly but radically redefining human nature. Three kinds of citizens exist in this society. There are engineers and managers who further the machine's program; these persons are favored with money and respect and make up the elite. A far larger class of people have been automated out of work; and these castoffs are segregated into a section of Ilium called Homestead. Then there is a small group of persons, such as barbers, whose special skills the computer has not yet gotten around to replacing.

Actually, no one counts in Ilium. All are phantom citizens. Many know that they are useless and others, the elite, are useful only by sufferance of the computer. One kind of citizen lives without hope; the other with anxiety. Where a computer sorts out human talents as data for solving the problems of life, people live in an emotional oblivion overlaid by a mechanized hierarchy. "'The smarter you are,'" in this society, "'the better you are.'" Feelings get in the way of progress. EPICAC XIV provides the new model for human nature; "wholly free of reason-muddying emotions," it can be "dead right about everything." *Dead* is the telling word. The machine annihilates whatever impedes its efficiency. When "'the machines can't stand him any more,'" as is the case with one engineer, the person is wiped out. Since humanity is competing with machines for survival, humanity's defeat is inevitable. The mind that created EPICAC XIV does not comprehend the basic moral truth that the human person may be very imperfect and yet worth a great deal. The compulsive technological mentality finds imperfection intolerable. Computerizing away the flaws in the human creature violates its nature and removes the very condition for growth. Standardization of this kind exposes humanity to the possibility of extinction.

The time and place of the story underscore the dehumanizing course of American life. The Foreword says that *"the characters are modeled after persons as yet unborn, or perhaps, at this writing, infants."* Since the main character is thirty-five and the time of writing is 1952, the time of the story would be 1987 or thereabouts. But fact has outdistanced fancy; the contemporary reader is likely to find *Player Piano* more dated than futuristic. As will hold true for all of Vonnegut's novels, a postwar memory recounts the events. World War II is vaguely recalled as "'clear back'"; and a bloodletting more anonymously labeled "the Last War" is ten years behind the nation. The action takes place around Ilium, New York, an imaginary city that is one of the upstate Greek revival towns, such as Ithaca, Syracuse, and Utica. Ilium is a transparently masked Schenectady, home of General Electric, maker of the better things for better living that Vonnegut promoted when he was a public relations man.

Vonnegut interchanges the fantastic with the factual to highlight technological assaults on the quality of everyday human existence. The name Ilium parodies the values of modern America by evoking the grand view of humans associated with the legendary Ilium (the other name for Troy). There is nothing about this Ilium to extol. The gallant hour of human history that the ancient city represents is over. Bureaucratic triviality has replaced grand undertaking; puny rivalry has stamped out great adventure; dreary sameness has supplanted mighty individuality. A tragic sense of the world has given way to an abusive, proprietary view of the environment. Life is no longer a contest between human beings and great forces. Fate once allowed for human choice impinging on the inexorable in a way that gave humanity a sense of personal destiny; but instead of Fate the latter-day Iliumites live under electronic determinism. This is the form of fate in our time. The way in which our age relates to ancient Greece is through violence; Ilium and legendary Troy both derive their identity from war. War gives Ilium a purpose for being. EPICAC XIV was born of war; and though the war that created it has ended, the computer continues to operate on the economic and social priorities of war. America has lived by the sword for so long that it has cynically accepted slaughter as inevitable and peace as an uneasy interregnum. No wonder Iliumites think in images of "the battlefield of life."

The psychological time of *Player Piano* is just such an awkward peace. Illusion about progress serves as ideology. "For once, after the great bloodbath of the war, the world really was cleared of unnatural terrors—mass starvation, mass imprisonment, mass torture, mass murder. Objectively, know-how and world law were getting their long-awaited chance to turn earth into an altogether pleasant and convenient place in which to sweat out Judgment Day." The moment is a postwar, pre-apocalyptic transition from the previous holocaust to the final one. Waiting for the end is the fate of Ilium, There is no ease. Dr. Paul Proteus, the novel's central figure, finds it "'just a hell of a time to be alive.'"

I I

Player Piano is the story of Dr. Proteus' sharpening awareness that, despite the official proclamation of sharing in a golden age, "the human situation was a frightful botch." His negative view of the system becomes a burden because it separates him from the securities he lives by. They are many, for, as manager of the Ilium Works, Dr. Proteus is rich and respected. In responding to what he sees as humanly degrading, Dr. Proteus undergoes a more radical change than his name foretells. From being a "personage," recognized and privileged, Paul Proteus becomes an "archcriminal," a disgraced nobody. In society's eyes the transformation is from a higher to a lower station, but Vonnegut leaves the reader with no doubt that for Paul Proteus, to live by his inner lights is moral growth.

He gains a new life. The process unfolds in three stages, which divide the novel in this way: disquiet (Chapters I-XIII), detachment (XIV-XXII), and expulsion (XXIII-end). The terms are negative because they describe Proteus' reaction against the culture he lives in. Proteus' establishing a new relation to the things of his life precipitates a re-creation of self, and that spiritual process constitutes the form of the novel. By equating Proteus' renewal with a humility rite, Vonnegut conveys his fundamental precept for life led under the boot of arrogance and power.

Doctor Paul Proteus—"Doctor" is just about the minimal evidence of the right to be a person in a world where brains set status—is the all-American man. Success is assured Proteus. The gifted son of a wartime leader and manager of the Ilium Works, he is slated to take over the larger Pittsburgh Works while on the way to the top of the organization. At the high tide of his career, a "nameless, aching need" nags him. The very vagueness of his disquiet indicates its importance. Initially, his sense of lack isolates him. "He'd felt for some time that everyone else in the system must be seeing something he was missing." When he gives a brief after-dinner talk to his colleagues, the disparity between his platitudinous salutes to how machines make "better goods for more people at less cost" and his personal feeling focuses his discontent. He knows that people pay for better material goods with their sense of worthiness. Those who cannot compete with the machines are remanded either to the Army or to the Reeks and Wrecks, the Reconstruction and Reclamation Corps, in which human hollowness is hidden. But even the technological elite, such as Proteus, lack "the sense of spiritual importance in what they were doing."

Paul is sick of paying. His "formless misgivings" assume a definite shape through two encounters. The first is a chance visit across the Iroquois River to Homestead, where live the masses whom the machine has automated out of work. Homestead is a terrifying place. Its squalors are spiritual. "'These displaced people need something, and the clergy can't give it to them,'" says the Reverend James J. Lasher to Paul Proteus. The apocryphal case of the boy who hanged himself because he "'couldn't find any good reason for being alive'" has the poignancy of truth. The abiding uselessness in Homestead erodes what little self-reliance the gadget-filled world has left these people. Without self-reliance the human species seems to be losing its ability to adapt to its own manufactured environment and preserve what is distinctly human. Humans are killing themselves by creating a synthetic milieu in which they cannot survive. Like the dinosaur and the saber-toothed tiger, humanity as we know and cherish it risks extinction. Culture is our special way of adapting to a new historic predic- ament. Culture is human ecology; and the emotional dearth in Ilium raises a question about people's ability to adapt to the mechanized en- vironment. The cultural past is dead to Iliumites. "'And what does an anthropologist do these days?'" Proteus asks. Nothing; or, since the whole human shebang seems to be going out of business, an anthropologist might try to excavate the vanishing present as a momento of human history. The Reeks and Wrecks are the links to the time when all people will be rendered extinct by the mechanistic evolution taking hold. What affects Proteus is not such a large notion as the end of humanity but the shared hopelessness he feels with the men across the river.

The second encounter that defines Proteus' misgiving is a private moral one. To get the promotion to Pittsburgh, he must lie about Lasher and Ed Finnerty, another friend, and turn them in as plotting to sabotage the Ilium Works. The bribe is made by Kroner, "the rock of faith in tech- nology," who embodies the fatuous dedication to progress that promotes sentimental cynicism. The order to be an informer outrages Proteus. He sees that in the name of patriotic preservation of the Works, Kroner will commission moral sabotage. Proteus' nameless need is for integrity, out of which his honest responses can flow.

Beyond the issue of honesty there is for Proteus the equally important trust of friendship. Finnerty is the first of Vonnegut's many secret agents, each of whom has "an air of mysteriousness about him, an implication that he knew of worlds unsuspected by anyone else—a man of unexplained absences and shadowy friends." Though a member of the prestigious National Industrial Planning Board, Finnerty detests "'this damn hierarchy that measures men against machines.'" A deeply lonely man, Finnerty takes to the edges of his mind where he gains a perspective on the mad, brutal doings at the center of modern American life. Finnerty takes pleasure in affronting the dreary tidiness of the managers and engineers with his unkempt style. He becomes a living critique of Ilium, as his very presence calls its values into question. But for Proteus, Finnerty's flam- boyant indifference is reassuring. Proteus looks for guidance to this bril- liant exception to the rules.

Initially, Finnerty's help is through emotional influence. He brings out Paul's loyalty to him, which encourages Paul to act on his grievance with society. Then, in the subtle way in which friends alter each other's point of view, Paul adopts his own kind of critical aloofness toward his colleagues and work. "At the beginning and close of each item of business he thought,

'To hell with you.'" Shifting his outlook from amusement to cynicism as the occasion requires, Paul Proteus makes his separate, momentary peace with the enemy around him—Proteus' being a mild form of the special psychic adjustments that we will see each of Vonnegut's major figures making to endure a wacky world. In *Player Piano,* to harbor a mere reservation about the goodness of this golden electronic age is unthinkable, even sinful, because in this America scientific progress is divine. Like Kronos, the king in the first golden age, Kroner presides over the rites of obedience. Kroner, who personifies an unalloyed faith in progress, cannot assimilate Paul's complaint over the spiritual disaster across the river in Homestead. "'I don't believe it came from your heart,'" Kroner decries. Kroner programs the loyalties of those he supervises in the same way that the computer edits reality by excluding what does not fit its program. Forced to hide his feelings, Proteus follows Finnerty's example by becoming an underground man—first discreetly, then actively.

Paul Proteus tries to dream his way out of the system. "He wanted to deal, not with society, but only with Earth as God had given it to man." The grand illusion of a simple life is as old as humanity. *Player Piano* is also concerned with this yearning. The associations are explicitly with Thoreau, who is cited appreciatively for preferring jail to supporting the Mexican War with his taxes. With Thoreau, and for much the same now-classical American reasons, Proteus looks to nature for a new life, a new container of self, to quicken the development of his consciousness. With the reluctant help of Doctor Pond, the Ilium real estate manager, he finds Gottwald (God's forest), a "microcosm of the past on the edge of Ilium." The abandoned farm offers Proteus a geographical separation that squares with his feeling of being outside Ilium's emotional limits. "It was a completely isolated backwater, cut off from the boiling rapids of history, society, and the economy. Timeless." God's forest, like God's planet Earth, is an irreparable ruin, but the discovery of each of the numerous inconveniences enhances Paul's daydream of living by the soil. Neither dry rot nor termites disenchant him. The reader, however, sees that the world as God created it has been plundered beyond rescue. The edifice of the farmhouse reveals the dilapidation of human history. The structure has shrunk to the point at which the rafters are inches above Paul's head. "The house seemed to have twisted and stretched on its foundations until it had found a position of comfort for all of its parts—like a sleeping dog." History cannot answer Paul's search for a way to live in a post-historical era. Like the house, human awareness has relieved its stresses through an unawakened sleep. There is no going back. The simple life is no longer possible. Gottwald is timeless in the sense of being destitute of time and consequently without the possibility of change; it is not timeless in the sense of being exempt from time's ravages.

Paul gives up the idea of retreating to nature. His "atavistic whim" is finally shattered by the responses of his wife Anita. The companion illusion to the pastoral ideal is the ideal of romantic love, and Paul has worked out in his mind how to reeducate Anita as a farmer's wife and supportive companion in the life of innocent harmony. And only wildly romantic love could envision Anita cavorting in the woodlawns. She has a "love for things colonial" but finds the authentic farm "'perfectly hideous'" because it is unmechanized. She likes her wood in Formica. Her idea of art is decorative. She wants pretty things around, but they must be useless—just as the system has made her a mere sexual ornament and appendage to her husband's career. In her own kitchen in Country Club, "a wooden butter churn held the door open, and clusters of Indian corn hung from the molding at aesthetic intervals." At Gottwald, in a flash of creativity, Anita sees how to improve on a dry-sink by putting a TV set in it. Her aesthetics reflect a larger moral insensitivity, which emerges in her cynical indifference to the misery of the Homesteaders. Paul recognizes that his marriage reinforces his self-denying relationship with the system. Anita is the corrupt system in female form. After the rural excursion Paul remains married but detaches himself emotionally from Anita just as he made a separate inner pact with the system.

Proteus passes through another version of the pastoral during his period of secret detachment. "Where the pine forest met the waters at the source of the St. Lawrence" is "the island called the Meadows." Like all woodland retreats, it is a place and a time apart. "The cream of the East and Middle West, engineering-wise and managerwise" is annually brought to the island by the organization as a reward for their loyalty in order to complete their personal development. One needs restraint in commenting on the Meadows because of its inherent excesses. Vonnegut is gentle with Gottwald because Proteus' need to escape and to love is genuine, despite his pursuing their fulfillment through illusion. Describing the Meadows, Vonnegut is broadly parodic because the corporate appropriation of our need for refreshment makes our environment and our lives bogus. The Meadows teases its visitors with a pastoral repose it does not provide. Men leave their families to spend two weeks amid the virgin forest on this island, but the complicated technocratic life they left is concealed on the Meadows, like the hidden loudspeaker that blares out orders to the guests. This green world does not bring the men away from their corrupt everyday lives, but deeper into it. The corporate mind infects nature. By comparison with the Meadows, a Boy Scout camp seems mature; a pro football game, serene; a rivival meeting, low-keyed. Fraternity, athletic competition, and religious conversion constitute what the corporate leaders believe is the best way to live. There are the Blue Team—"'Oh you Blue Team, you tried and true team'"—and the Green Team, the *Song Book* providing salutes to the "common-law brotherhood" sealed "of their having shared so much beauty, excitement, and deep emotion together," and solemn swearings to "'uphold the honor of my profession.'" That the Meadows is regarded as a model world comments on the poverty of mind conceiving the utopian dispensation. Vonnegut is showing his impatience with the impulse to found ideal places that sacrifice our actual community. Looking for the paradisal, Proteus finds a disintegrating Gottwald. Sent to the Meadows for renewal, he meets the infernal. The Green Team has a placard inside its building that parodies Dante's warning over the entrance to hell. "'Abandon All Hope, Ye Who Don't Wear Green Shirts!'" The adolescent ballyhoo tips us off to Vonnegut's view of the entire forlorn place as sinister.

The rituals at the Meadows vivify the lies of community and belief that are fostered in the men. Two are noteworthy. Every summer Kroner, the boss, honors those who died during the previous year. The guests gather around the Oak, which doubles as a symbol of the strength of the national organization, for a memorial service. This summer the Service pays tribute to Doctor Ernest S. Bassett, whose rank "'at the head of the procession of civilization'" is secured by an unspecified contribution to better living at less cost. Now, the gathering of men around trees goes back to primitive times; and the oak in particular is esteemed as a sacred object, a Golden Bough from which the dying god is regenerated. The ancient cultic god was slain to create new life. Vonnegut makes use of his anthropological knowledge to sharpen his fictive attack on the pretensions of a civilized society that is really barbarous. Norbert Wiener's grave warning not to confuse "know-how" with "know-what" comes to mind. The modern reenactment includes slayings without purpose. Death itself has neither mystery nor dignity. Kroner is a profane priest who makes a mystic ceremony into a public relations stunt, just as the oracular oak has been diminished to a catchy symbol on the organization's letterhead and to a stage prop in a heavy-handed play by Bill Holdermann.

The play is the second corrupting rite. Vonnegut provides the full script; and having the play form within the novel form deepens our sense that life in a technocracy is acted out according to a scenario for living. Exaggerated as the dialogue is, the utterances are not more chauvinistic, nor more stereotypical than are, say, the serious remarks of Kroner or Anita. That the piece borrows from the medieval morality play further establishes the dogmatic view of life and of art in this society. The play presents the struggle between Radical and an allegorized antagonist called *"a clean-cut, handsome young engineer"* for the loyalty of Mr. John Averageman. Telling the story even once would be redundant. We know it already from our popular culture, comic strips, and soap operas. Its style is its meaning. The level of political intelligence of the playwright equals that of the Kate Smith war-bond shows of World War II. The playwright's creative imagination approaches (but does not attain) that of kindergarten show-and-tell. Medieval drama's didactic intention of honest clarity is coarsened into finger-pointing dogmatism. Everyman's life touched on the great issue of redemption; Averageman's life is a matter of economic consumption.

Paul sees his part in this childish spectacle and wants out. A light flashes in his eyes; and like the Apostle Paul on the road to Damascus, Paul Proteus' conscience is awakened and he is converted. When his superiors order him to infiltrate the rebellious Ghost Shirt Society, which Finnerty has by now joined, Paul angrily tries to quit. "'I quit, I quit, I quit.'" His anger is frustrated by the organization's taking his quitting as a clever cover for their cabal. If Paul cannot quit (resigning implies a free choice), he can revolt and he does. There results a rapid divestiture of Proteus' public self. A bartender denies him a bourbon and water; Anita deserts him; a cop strips him of his identification cards; and a keyboard punches out his biography for the police. Each of the revocations bringing about Paul's protean self-change exposes the false basis of social justice, love, law, and self-respect that technology has affected. Paradoxically, Paul's fall from official grace allows him to "become merely a man." *Merely* is the crucial word here. It signifies "not otherwise than," or "purely" man. Vonnegut's gentle irony carries a momentous critique of the superhuman ideas the machine has imposed on our lives which, ironically, underscore our sense of insignificance. Vonnegut's defense of humanity begins, then, with an acceptance of our imperfection. To be more than human implies that being *merely a man* is not enough. *Player Piano* demonstrates the necessity of demythologizing just such fake enlargements of ourselves.

III

The Ghost Shirts, a secret society, want to effect a backward movement by replacing machines with people. Their efforts are doomed. The society's name, Vonnegut the anthropologist accurately explains, comes from the American Indian Ghost Dance movement of the 1890s when the red men tried futilely to protect themselves from annihilation by white men's guns by wearing magic shirts. They danced to recreate the old, simple world destroyed by the whites. Fantasy can create fantasy worlds and check fantasy bullets, but the whites dealt with the actual stuff. The failure of the Ghost Dance, as James Mooney shows in *The Ghost Dance,*[2] marks the collapse of American Indian culture. The Indian predicament in the late nineteenth century evidences the historical point *Player Piano* has been challenging the reader with all along, namely, that the human species goes out on the evolutionary limb of extinction when it cannot adapt to a new environment. Though the method proved inadequate, the impulse behind the Ghost Dance derives from the energy that does allow people to survive. Weston La Barre's *The Ghost Dance: The Origins of Religion* places the 1890s movement in the large context of crisis cults in order to explain how it was an expression of the basic human need for belief.[3] Believing, which is a distinctly human phenomenon, makes humans human and determines how and whether they endure.

The modern Ghost Shirts of Ilium are dupes of history. They too fight hardware with fantasy. They deal in such absolutes as "History," which sanctions their "righteous and determined" plan to set off a revolution complete with a messiah. The leaders are willing to accept inevitable defeat because revolting for the sake of the record makes the catastrophe worthwhile.

Paul's participation in the revolt measures the meaning of the Society and marks the final stage of his growth. After slipping dream-inducing pentathol into his bourbon, the members elect Paul the messiah. A new grandiosity attends his newest self: from superperson Works Manager to a nobody to the anointed savior of the whole works. The dream is nightmarish. Paul, the arrested archcriminal, feels euphoric over the new cause he has taken up. Whether conformist or traitor, Paul is "a glib mouthpiece for a powerful, clever organization." The self remains a marionette, the phantom piano player—but not totally vanquished. Here is Paul during his trial for treason, wired like a puppet to a lie-detector, interrogated, gazing into the television camera, trying to defend himself: "'The most beautiful

peonies I ever saw ... were grown in almost pure cat excrement. I—'"
Goodness comes from sordidness; beauty and life from waste. The image
argues for the imperfect mixture of higher and lower impulses that is our
nature. If Paul serves any messianic purpose, it lies in his attempt to deliver
his fellow Iliumites from that idolatrous technology which makes their
imperfection an evil. He tries to free the mind from its enslaving notion of
perfection.

The ending of *Player Piano* leaves the reader with precisely the con-
trariety of new birth arising from catastrophe. The revolt has taken place.
Ilium is "a world of ruins." "Bodies lay everywhere, in grotesque attitudes
of violent death, but manifesting the miracle of life in a snore, a mutter,
the flight of a bubble from the lips." The narrative ends by duplicating
the battlefield image with which it began. The revolution fails. After
wrecking practically everything in sight, the masses instinctively proceed
to repair an Orange-O machine. The crowd rejoices when they get it going
again. The machine is cranked up. Though the revolutionary cause is com-
promised, the human spirit is affirmed by the mob's sense of being useful.
The hilarity beneath the surface of momentous events guarantees the
genuineness of their celebration. Paul, with the other leaders, turns himself in to the authorities, disillusioned but not bitter. At the end, he is not
a saboteur but a witness to many kinds of human folly. The final words
are Lasher's, spoken "almost gaily" as he lashes out at attempts to halt
revolutionary progress: "'Forward March.'" As Paul realizes when he is
arrested, "the denouement was still to come." We strive for ultimates because, unlike the spring flowers mentioned in the novel's epigraph from
Matthew 6:28, we do not have the connatural wisdom to live by faith,
which relieves our inevitable anxiety over the future.

Vonnegut provides a running subplot in *Player Piano* which dramatizes
the freshness of viewpoint that we are to adopt toward these astonishing
doings. The Shah of Bratpuhr, the "wizened and wise" guru of the six-
million-strong Kolhouri sect, along with his aide Khashdrahr Miasma,
comes "to see what he could learn in the most powerful nation on earth
for the good of his people." What we call good derives from how we define
human. In America, goods stand for the good. The Shah is schooled in
amplidgnes, cryostats, hairdryers, zymometers. *"Nibo!"* (nothing) he
cries while being wisked off in an ammo truck away from the latest American revolution. EPICAC XIV cannot solve the problem of suffering. The
old riddle in insoluble. There may be history but there is no spiritual progress. *"Brahouna!* Live!'" pronounces the Shah as he flees the hazardous

country he was to model his backward country on. He seems to speak for Vonnegut and to act as he would. The Shah has learned how to laugh at gruesome realities. Detached amusement is a useful way to quiet the heart in times of misery; and laughter, we shall come to see, is the method that Vonnegut brings to a position of structural determination as he matures as a novelist.

We can prepare ourselves to understand Vonnegut's development by pausing briefly to reflect on his treatment in his first novel of the suffering that is so unfathomable that we are invited to chuckle futilely over it. Though the novel unmistakably blames the terrible state of life on an unbridled application of technology, it implies a more fundamental reason for the problem in its analysis of the human mind. The allusions to the divine Titan and Olympian names of Kronos and Proteus go beyond describing personality traits in Dr. Kroner and Dr. Proteus; they point to the impulse in the modern technological mind to be an autonomous force like God, who alone has the power to create. The novel amuses us with the puny effort of the countless branches of the Works uniting to change creation as though God's work required perfecting. But the novel also intends to startle us with something sinister. Aspiring toward moral autonomy violates the order of creation. In grabbing for the complete freedom of God, the technological mind abuses the freedom God has given the human creature to share in life within limitations. The consequence of this overreaching is the degradation and oppression felt by all the figures in the story.

In *Player Piano* humanity lives under the curse brought about by its own arrogance. The novels that follow take the reader to many remote, exotic places as they recount the adventures of many wonderfully strange persons; and yet they come back to this old—Old Testament, really—predicament of the fundamental break in the relationship among persons and between them and their universe. This condition gives rise to and is set over against the parallel theme of Vonnegut's novels, namely: How shall humanity enter a free and fruitful life? The charming Shah of Bratpuhr is onto something when he shouts "'Live!'" Celebration too is Vonnegut's subject.

2

THE SIRENS OF TITAN

> But if ill-will or the desire to hurt others should
> stir your mind, purify it again with its opposite,
> which will act on it like a wishing jewel on
> muddied water.
>
> From a Buddhist meditation

"'Live!'" urges Malachi Constant, the main figure in *The Sirens of Titan* (1959), as he tries to convince his son of the wisdom of leaving inhospitable Mars. Constant is repeating the advice given by the Shah of Bratpuhr in *Player Piano* (1952), and the direct echo of Vonnegut's first novel in the second locates the thematic foundation of his rich career. The narrative line of Vonnegut's first two novels traces the way the hero makes his path through worlds that check his decent impulses, finally to be cleansed by a restoration of the human values that had been sacrificed. Both books show the need for a new human beginning. In *Player Piano*, Paul Proteus rebels against the technological violation of humanity, and in *The Sirens of Titan*, Malachi Constant reacts against his own debauchery; but what is constant for Paul and protean for Malachi is the final commitment to compassion and to life in all its unpredictability.

There are, however, between Vonnegut's first two books, telling differences in mode and in moral penetration of their common theme. By and large, *Player Piano* is a traditionally composed novel. Though Vonnegut uses nonsense, creates a nonlanguage, tries his hand at word catalogues, his technique is not in the end experimental. The anthropological material is not esoteric, and the novel's futurism and anti-utopian satire leave our imagination unchallenged. The setting of Paul Proteus' renunciation of the political system is on recognizable Earth. Now these energies are also in *The Sirens of Titan*, but they swing out more widely and plumb deeper. The second novel sweeps cosmically through the solar system and depicts those outer worlds not satirically, but with visionary celebration. Moreover, the moral compass takes in spiritual principles of retribution that lay deeper than the political effects brought about by Proteus' rebellion.

The Sirens of Titan presents a new feeling for fiction which has challenged our critical vocabulary. James Mellard, in his distinguished essay on Vonnegut's early practice, argues that with his second book Vonnegut moves into a "new mode"[1] of fiction. That new mode derives from a contemporary, McLuhanesque adaptation of ancient oral literature such as the folk tale. The result is a re-creation of an acoustical model made of "a mosaic of styles."[2] Mellard analogizes from Northrop Frye's discussion of naive literature[3] to show how Vonnegut's treatment gives new meaning to the old formulaic mode. Other readers have commented on the innovative quality of *The Sirens of Titan*. Karen and Charles Wood see it as a "space opera."[4] The science-fiction material, for Peter Reed, provides a basis for Vonnegut's traditional exploration of "existential 'whys.' "[5] Jerome Klinkowitz judges the novel "one of Vonnegut's most sophisticated experiments in literary art."[6]

Whatever view one takes of the inventiveness of *The Sirens of Titan*, the crucial issue is the form that arises from Vonnegut's peculiar handling of his space odyssey. In fact, when Vonnegut's art is discredited, it is usually on the belief that his novels are pulp exercises without meaningful shape. This is the gist of Charles Thomas Samuels's 1971 attack in the *New Republic*, where he flatly dismisses Vonnegut as a "bogus talent" that lends itself to the ready, uncritical affection of adolescent readers.[7] The charge deserves an answer; and though there are many intelligent appreciations of Vonnegut's work, none has sought to show analytically the formal side of his achievement. *The Sirens of Titan* is the best place to begin the demonstration. Though only his second novel, it signals a clear advance over the first. It has reached the large popular audience for which Vonnegut wrote it, and yet subtly works through patterns that we associate with his more recent and acclaimed books.

The novel's *cri-de-coeur*—"'Live!'"—expresses our most primal human need and implies that the universe is set against our fulfilling such a need. Where the struggle to make the most of life is the theme of *Player Piano*, in *The Sirens of Titan* it becomes the form. With all its cosmic range, the story is told with a pointed simplicity. The choice of a popular manner underscores the universality of Constant's desire to be free and to be decent. The simplest message is given in the simplest way. Naive literature is one name for this treatment; parable is another, and in this case is more apt because it conveys the moral tone underlying the tale. The nature of the parable is such that meaning can readily be extracted from it. This is the effect Vonnegut seeks. He even tells brief stories within the novel and conspicuously draws the lessons for us to show us how to read his novel as a whole. But paradoxes, bewilderments, and reversals in the total story make any single extrapolation seem inadequate. That the story is not reducible to a statement of its meaning is its distinctiveness. What we have is a sophisticated treatment of the naive genre. *The Sirens of Titan* is *almost* a parable. Though it bids us to live all we can, the events acknowledge impediments to doing so. The necessity of accommodating to chance is part of the lesson, which is a way of saying that the novel exemplifies how we live now amid astonishing forces that dislocate us from our centers of identification. Vonnegut's second book is about such displacements on an astronomical scale. By following the erratic course of Malachi Constant's interplanetary wandering, we can trace the changes in his human aspects, for cosmic is not only a geographic designation in the novel but as well a measurement of the hero's inner human expanse.

After an epigraph ("I guess somebody up there likes me") that guardedly salutes wholesome trust in providence, the tale begins in the colloquial accents of the old-fashioned storyteller:

Everyone now knows how to find the meaning of life within himself.
But mankind wasn't always so lucky. Less than a century ago men and women did not have easy access to the puzzle boxes within them.
They could not name even one of the fifty-three portals to the soul.

The plain syntax suggests values of simplicity and community, which the action will affirm. Just as the parable is the simplest form in which to express the simplest lesson, so the loose declarative sentence is the simplest grammatical structure. It so dominates the novel that it becomes formulaic, achieving at times the quality of a chant. The style speaks for artlessness and the commonplace. The narrative voice provides signals to the audience for the stance it should take, and here Vonnegut expects nothing more of the reader than would the modes of communication in the popular culture. The voice is the kind, knowing, legendary one of, say, fairy tales.

Hans Christian Andersen begins "The Nightingale" by reminding us that the story of the Emperor of China needs retelling: "It happened a good many years ago, but that's just why it's worthwhile to hear the story, before it is forgotten." Vonnegut adopts a version of the once-upon-a-time formula to create a sense of innocent wonder through which the lesson of the tale will emerge. The voice reminisces about the future to see where we are now. Where we are is in moral dispossession. The condition is not new. Our human history is the history of our separation from our human rights. Nor is there a shortage of parables on the subject. Genesis 3, recounting Adam's and Eve's ejection from Eden, is a parable of alienation. But Vonnegut's parable expands the dimensions of human alienation from God to all his creation, the universe. Yet the patriarchal tone reassures the reader of a final reconciliation. "Everyone now knows. . . ." "For reasons as yet mysterious. . . ." "It is grotesque for anyone as primitive as an Earthling to explain. . . ." This persistent self-confident style recommends the homey, even corny, truths underlying the plainest truth of life, to live. The openhearted voice articulates the mystery and value of life at a time when life seems mortally threatened. Complementing this moral freshness are a wry detachment and a wise-cracking self-consciousness. These witty tones come through in the borrowings of stock characters from kitsch, such as comic strips and movie serials. In this novel Buck Rogers and Captain Marvel fly again as Mars invades Earth and allegorical figures engage in daring pursuits and passionate romance. There are spectacular materializations of people, and sudden dematerializations.

If the voice Vonnegut develops in *The Sirens of Titan* is folksy, it is also complex. The rhetorical gestures express a double mood. Set against the plain manner, but serving the same purpose—to communicate directly to a common reader—is a superlative idiom. Here we find Vonnegut the pop writer trying to give another kind of art a break by giving dignity to the petty experience of contemporary life. The parable tells of the richest American, who, as the son of "'the luckiest man who ever lived,'" has "wallowed in every known form of voluptuous turpitude" and must atone for his hedonism by taking a pilgrimage as excessive as his sins. Since his transgressions are vast, he becomes a space wanderer, the supreme pilgrim. In the course of his expiation the "playboy of the Solar System" encounters "the highest-paid executive in the country," the most powerful man in the cosmos, and "the most handsome, healthy, clean-minded specimen" of another planet. And still more: this most profligate man rapes the most haughty, aristocratic woman on Earth and finally falls totally in love with her. Together with their wild, savage son, they live in bliss. These extravagances go into making this billionaire rake "'the most memorable, magnificent, and meaningful human being of modern times.'"

Oh-ing and ah-ing before such giantism go hand in hand with contemporary folk fantasy. This is what Saturday-movie matinees and Disney are all about. The exaggeration allows Vonnegut gently to satirize the material he uses. What is especially noteworthy is how Vonnegut gives meaning to what in other hands would be mere bravura devices. Conventional science fiction presents the spectacle of enormity and of the outer world to dazzle us by honoring technology. Its verisimilitude requires that we suspend our disbelief. Not so with Vonnegut. His exaggerations make us stay aware of this tale as fiction, as imagined. For him, space exploration ventures into possibilities, not facts; and the possibilities are those of inner spiritual zones, not of a fake mechanism or fixed cosmography. At the outset of the novel the narrator says of the time when the action occurs:

> Outwardness lost, at last, its imagined attractions.
> Only inwardness remained to be explored.
> Only the human soul remained *terra incognita*.

Vonnegut uses science fiction the way Romantic poets used classical mythology: to amaze us with the cosmic dimensions of human nature. It is a common, not to say at this time in literary history, banal, theme.

I I

The marvel that is the subject of *The Sirens of Titan* is the humanization of Malachi Constant of Hollywood, California, who has three billion dollars but is a spiritual pauper. He nevertheless evolves into a good man because his dissoluteness contains the seed of his virtue. In the beginning of the parable he lives in corruption. By passing through the *terra incognita* of his soul he comes out into magnificence. Spiritual transformation is the message that Malachi, whose name in Hebrew means "messenger of the Lord," delivers to the world. Squalor and glory are twin aspects of his capacity to become. Becoming is what makes Malachi constant. The extreme quality of his transformation is the parabolist's way of drawing a sharp lesson. If this billionaire rake can do it, we all can. Constant's reversal comes about through a process of his nature being brought into moral balance. Balance is a universal principle of moral life: a life shall be rendered for a life, an eye for an eye; punishment should fit the crime; and so on. We saw previously how Vonnegut balances a plain with a superlative manner, a naive story with literary sophistication, and satire with serious tones. Embodied in the character of Malachi Constant, the principle of balance takes on the ethical quality of correcting a fault through its opposite. Balance pervades *The Sirens of Titan*. It is the theme, the manner, and the principle of its form, which is to say that the novel's form is Constant's act of living. This is still another way of saying that the book is about justice.

And about love, which *The Sirens of Titan* is very much concerned with. In the first chapter, while Constant is bragging about all the women he has had, he comes upon a photograph in his wallet of a woman whom he has not conquered. It was slipped behind the picture of Miss Canal Zone, Constant's latest triumph. He looks closely and sees a lovely snapshot of a clear coral bay where three women pose, one white, one gold, one brown. "They looked up at Constant, begging him to come to them, to make them whole with love." These beauties from the White Rock soda pop ad are the sirens in the book's title. They are the call to the sex-filled, love-starved Malachi Constant. Constant's answer to their call is the story. The man who has lived by lust learns how to love. In doing so *he* is made whole. Love balances by piecing out his emotional divisions.

In keeping with his desire to reach a large popular readership, Vonnegut vivifies Constant's trip into the inner *terra incognita* of love through the great contemporary mythic voyage, the space odyssey. (A Joyce or a Proust would use the less accessible metaphor of mental association to chart the route into the psyche's unknown areas.) Constant flies from Earth, to Mars, to Mercury, back to Earth, on to Titan, and finally back to Earth. The stopping places are far out, but the excursion is merely an enlargement of the way everyone who lives in time moves. Winston Niles Rumfoord, who knows a great deal about space and time, says to his wife that " 'life for a punctual person is like a roller coaster.' " The contour of Constant's voyage proves his point: the ups, the dips, the turns are all there; and the time-caught person rides it out. The path of the roller coaster pictures times spatially, and one can see the whole life-course at once. Blocked out this way, events appear accidental, pointless, beyond our control. The roller coaster, then, is fate. No wonder many characters, who are caught in a swirl, ask for clues " 'on what life might be about.' "

Near the end of the book Rumfoord himself is baffled. "'I should still like to know just what the main point of this Solar System episode has been.'" Chance governs all—not mind, not providence, not conscience. Still, as in the fairy tale, *The Sirens of Titan* turns out absolutely right. By observing how the principle of balance operates on Constant in each of the places he visits, we can see how randomness makes sense as debauchery is corrected.

The novel's first three chapters describe life on Earth as it was between World War II and the Third Great Depression. Life is a lavish mess. U. S. A., Earth, Solar System, Milky Way are overstuffed with goods, and "'there is nothing more that anybody wants the factories to make because everybody already has two, three, and four of everything.'" Malachi Constant of Hollywood epitomizes the human emptiness that the junk of consumerism is manufactured to fill. He is shown, after one of his fifty-six-day parties, dressed in blue-green evening shorts with a gold brocade dinner jacket, dead drunk in the gutter of his kidney-shaped swimming pool. His spectacular pool is one of the many images of a costly, funereal receptacle of trash in the parable. Next to his blue rhinestone telephone booth, the pool has a blanket of gardenias pushed to the side by the party's rubble—a TV set, a hypodermic syringe, a busted white grand piano, and more. It is a collage of the things we live by. The narrator points a warning finger at the scene, calling it "a punchbowl in hell." Ranson K. Fern, the chief executive for Constant's vast enterprises, describes the situation well. "'When you get right down to it, everybody's having a perfectly lousy time of it, and I mean everybody. And the hell of it is, nothing seems to help much.'"

Winston Niles Rumfoord of Newport, Rhode Island, has a scheme to help his fellow Earthlings out. On Mars, Rumfoord is mobilizing an army of invaders to attack Earth. When they do, Earthlings will be brought together by a common purpose. The scheme includes the founding of the Church of God of the Utterly Indifferent to make the new solidarity permanent. This religion will remove the illusion that luck is God's handiwork and so obviate people's foolish attempts to please him. The outrageousness of Rumfoord's scheme measures how desperate is life on Earth. Once every fifty-nine days he materializes in Newport. His most recent materialization is the first event of the novel. Constant is formally invited to witness Rumfoord's appearance because the classy Newport scion has plans for the "notorious rakehell" who has been making "mankind look bad." Before being snared by the Martian agents Helmholtz and Miss Wiley, Constant takes an economic nose dive on the roller coaster of chance. His financial empire, the conglomerate Magnus Opus, falls apart. The richest man becomes penniless. But only in material poverty can Constant's spiritual trip be taken. The journey into outer space instructs Constant and the reader in the true nature of his affluent abyss, without the illusions adopted to make it tolerable.

III

Mars (Chapters 4-7). In astrology Mars rules over the principle of action, which involves aggression and passion. Rumfoord, who controls Mars, has negated the planet's energy by turning it into a war machine. Every aspect of Martian life reflects the human instinct for devastation, imported from Earth. On this planet human aggression has been brought to its uttermost degree.

As is customary during passages into the beyond, the voyager undergoes an initiatory rite to forget the world he left behind. The Martian welcome is out of a Frankenstein movie—the new arrival goes to the hospital to have a radio antenna inserted under the crown of his skull. The antenna keeps everyone in line by an electronic pain that commands all behavior. The operation makes a lobotomy look like benign therapy, and is efficient in moving the war preparations along. In effect, Mars brings about its own brutal kind of equality. The control box is manned by Boaz, the "brown Hercules," who as a black Earthling was powerless but who now pulls the switches. The amnesia operation levels down all the twelve thousand displaced Earthlings to automatons. The first glimpse of Mars is, appropriately, that of a ten-thousand-man infantry-division machine, chanting as one.

Constant, who "had everything back on Earth," is on Mars a lowly private. His new name is gratuitously conferred—"something like *Pops,* or *Gramps,* or *Unk.*" After discharge from the hospital, Unk's first act is to strangle his old friend, Stony Stevenson, who is chained to a stake. The murder epitomizes the naked nihilism on Mars. Chapter Four, which opens the Mars sequence, is a series of sentences, clipped and loose, to convey the mental blankness out of which Unk is acting. The emotional deadness around Unk—the zombie eyes that are "as empty as the windows of abandoned textile mills"—shows him the life he led on Earth. His aggressive amassing of companies, his use of money as power over others, his insensitivity are all clarified before his eyes. On Earth he pursued pleasure; on Mars he must learn pain. *"The more pain I train myself to stand, the more I learn,"* he writes in a letter to himself. Unk is further immersed in a social system based on the selfish separation in which he lived. On Mars people *"learned to get along all alone."* No one misses anyone. No one thinks of anyone.

Like Dante, Unk is a privileged visitor to the other world. He participates in the life of the future state only to the degree required for him to learn its moral lesson and is, therefore, exempt from its fatal finality. So the operation to hollow out his memory does not take fully and he begins to miss his wife Bee and his son Chrono. Unk comes to perceive the moral deadness of Mars. For once his imagination opens out to others as he dreams of taking his family to some peaceful place. "'Mars is a very bad place for love, a very bad place for a family man, Unk,'" warns Rumfoord in disguise. Unk comprehends that Mars is just a bad place. Captive to self-indulgence on Earth, Unk is held captive to brutality on Mars.

Self-indulgence and brutality are twin sides of destruction. In Hollywood we saw Constant destroying himself from within. On Mars we see disaster organized into an economic and social system. Though ostensibly preparing to invade Earth, the Martians are really setting up their own destruction. Their suicidal destiny constitutes the parabolist's warning about such an unfeeling, war-producing and self-centered life. All except a favored few are killed when Mars invades Earth. Bellicose as the Martians are, they cannot match the butchering talents of Earthlings. With the likes of Mrs. Lyman R. Peterson of Boca Raton, Florida, on the front lines, Mars has no chance. She picks off the invaders with her son's .22 as they step out of their space ship in her back yard. In its ability to kill, the planet devoted to aggression comes in second to Earth.

Mercury (Chapters 8-9). Unk and Boaz are chosen by Rumfoord to be spared the death trip. Instead, they are detoured to Mercury for three years of safekeeping for additional learning. Mercury rules intellect in its broadest sense, which takes in not only the power of the mind but also the various seen and unseen modes of communication. Here, as with Mars, Vonnegut works through astrological influence and underscores Mercury's significance by making it sing all the time. The planet is made up of deep caves, which enhance its envelope of musical enchantment. Within these dwell Mercury's only life—lovely aquamarine creatures that are membranes about a foot high and eight inches wide, kite-like, built to receive the acoustical vibrations of the atmosphere for nourishment.

On their four suction-cups they creep to wherever the song is richest on Mercury. Called *harmoniums*, their name describes not only their life as music receivers but also the total harmonic concord of Mercury. As a void, Mercury exposes the solipsism Constant and Boaz endured on Earth; and as a singing sphere, it offers the possibility of pure contact beyond language. The two marooned space travelers learn how to get out of themselves to life outside the self in a way appropriate to the individual capacity of each. They are schooled in emotional harmony.

Boaz comes to be perfectly at home on Mercury. He loves the harmoniums, devoting his life to sustaining theirs. Like Kurtz and Lord Jim, who deal with an alien environment by dominating it, Boaz becomes "God Almighty to the harmoniums." A favored harmonium is allowed the ecstasy of feeding on his pulse. The relation between Boaz and the harmoniums has perfect communication. Nothing is lost between them; what is felt *is* the message. Lord Boaz calls the message love, in an illusion that makes his life good. "'Don't *truth* me,'" he muses, "'and I won't *truth* you.'" If truth is that which makes people happy, then Boaz achieves ecstatic certitude. "Not to be lonely, not to be scared—Boaz had decided that those were the important things in life." By believing in his imagined rapport with the harmoniums, Boaz is made whole. The symbiosis provides connection and courage. Fittingly, he remains on Mercury, where he lives in the illusion of love. Love is a benediction for his trust in illusion, and transforms Mercury's vibration into Boaz's eschaton.

Not so with Unk, who "was at war" with Mercury's environment. He finds the harmoniums "'obscenely unmotivated, insensitive, and dull,'" as Dr. Frank Minot describes them in *Are Adults Harmoniums?* He is outraged by Boaz's blatant projections of humanity on these unresponsive membranes and tries in a moment of insanity to murder Boaz when he brings "'a cute little feller'" into their space ship. Boaz's imagined relations with the harmoniums deride Constant's actual yearning for Bee, Chrono, and Stony. On Mercury, the planet of the mind, Constant is driven out of his own mind, as he was driven out of his home on Earth. He wants communication based on human community, which means mutuality and imperfection. This is Mercury's lesson for Constant. Its perfection reveals its inadequacy: pure communication is pure mind, which is deprived of the give-and-take, the vital tension that brings person in touch with person.

Earth-Titan-Earth (Chapters 10-12). And so back to Earth, where Rumfoord's Church of God of the Utterly Indifferent has taken hold. Unk does not, however, find the planet as he left it. Though he does not recognize the situation, Unk sees people aspiring toward the sheer unthinking harmony of Mercury. People have been reduced to harmoniums. "When the bell was rung madly, the parishioners were to feel ecstasy" and come and greet the glorious appearance of the Space Wanderer whom Rumfoord sets up as a messiah, just as Paul Proteus was in *Player Piano*. Earth seems a perfect place. Unk arrives in the perfect season, spring, to the rhythm of the perfect spring-song that begins *The Canterbury Tales*, *"Whan that Aprille with his shoures sote...."* The chant of new life voices the harmony of justice established by the new religion. Each person takes on a handicap that offsets his or her advantage in life in order to make "the race of life . . . fair." Some wear bags of lead weight. The beautiful might wear frumpy clothes; the intelligent might marry the stupid. "And what made them all so happy was that nobody took advantage of anybody anymore." Each according to his or her handicap. Constant has left pure communication for pure justice, which makes life marvelous, but also makes life false to the very distinctions the eye sees as true.

Earth after the Martian war is turned inside out. Now that there is no hierarchy based on power, the man of privilege, Malachi Constant, serves as the image of "a repellent way of life that was no more." Wealth is alchemized into weal. There are three billion followers. (Malachi had a fortune of three billion dollars.) The just new Earth incorporates all of Constant's history as allegorized in his moral journey so far. The correction of his abuse of power on Earth, the forgetfulness of the past and individual differences of Mars, and the vibrating harmony of Mercury are institutionalized by Rumfoord's new religion. "When Rumfoord staged a passion play," the parabolist gently warns the reader, "he used nothing but real people in real hells." For his brave new world Rumfoord has mounted a spectacle of abiding purgation, an Earth atoning for its record of inequality. A reader familiar with Dante will think of the use of the counterweight of stones to humble the proud souls in the *Purgatorio* (Cantos X-XI). Constant's role in this high drama, like Paul Proteus' in *Player Piano*, is to be a marvel, a lesson and not a person. Once again he is a captive, now to the script of Rumfoord's religious drama. Humbled, with his gaze "lowered," Constant is exiled to Titan with Bee and Chrono. The little family gets the Great Good Place it sought, and Earth is cleansed of its "central symbol of wrong-headedness."

Titan is "a warm and fecund moon of Saturn." Saturn governs the principle of safety, and that is what the family achieves on this satellite.

Titan's security gives Constant the gratification that his money could not buy. "Constant was self-sufficient. He raised or gathered or made everything he needed." In his seventies he matures into a comforting "sweet" old man who, at long last, falls in love with Bee. And in keeping with the moral symmetry of the parable, Bee undergoes her own reversal from a haughty aristocrat to a tender wife. Chrono too has mellowed. "'Thank you, Mother and Father,'" shouts the reformed delinquent as he takes off with the Titanic bluebirds, "'for the gift of life.'" Chrono speaks for the entire family, whose harmony derives from the total agreement of the energies of creation on Titan. On this moon, "Life," says the parabolist in rejoicing wonder, "was but a soaring dream."

Though the tale of Constant's fulfilling his humanity is at an end, and the ending strikes the chord of the happily-ever-after resolution, the novel has not ended, has not fulfilled its energies. Vonnegut does not leave the reader with the image of a charmed life on enchanting Titan. The simplicity of this simple story has its ambivalence. For one thing, Rumfoord comes to realize his captivity by a greater power. The wizard of Newport is ruled by Tralfamadore, a planet from another galaxy with a civilization and technology millions of years advanced beyond anything in the solar system. Salo, a tangerine-colored Tralfamadorian messenger, has been calling the shots by generously giving Rumfoord half of his UWTB, the Universal Will to Become. Together they designed life on Mars, its invasion of Earth, and the subsequent ruling form of belief. Truth to tell, the whole shebang comes about because Salo needs a spare part for his crippled space ship. This disclosure of a trivial first cause of life shatters any frame of reference that we might use to explain the principle activating solar life. Vonnegut gives a new genesis. The expansion of the universe and the evolution of Earth have not directed civilization. Nor does human history culminate it. What Earth regards as civilization amounts to a mere interlude in the central story of Tralfamadore message-sending. Stonehenge spells out a message that the replacement part is on its way to Salo; the Great Wall of China gives a message of reassurance to Salo that he has not been forgotten. The view of our universe from Tralfamadore offers the put-down as cosmology, an experience more humbling than Constant's repentance because it applies to all humanity. Bewildered by these revelations, Rumfoord asks his crony, Salo, the question that is on the reader's mind: "'I should still like to know just what the main point of this Solar System episode has been.'"

One answer has already been suggested. The universe is a caprice operating independently of any order or of any scheme the human mind can project onto it. "'Luck,'" Rumfoord says, "'is the way the wind swirls and the dust settles eons after God has passed by.'" Constant's roller coaster trip vivifies the wake left by God's vacating the world. His personal history bears witness to chance before the new believers in chaos. "I WAS A VICTIM OF A SERIES OF ACCIDENTS, AS ARE WE ALL." The further we go into outer space, the more trivial the universe becomes, until finally, beyond the rim from Tralfamadore, it all becomes a joke, a shaggy-dog story that tediously adds pointless afterthoughts.

The cosmos may be a joke, even a dirty joke, as the mentality of our time believes, but Vonnegut figures Constant's conversion as a living response to Rumfoord's quandary. Speaking of falling in love with Bee very late in their life together, Constant avows to Salo, "'It took us that long to realize that a purpose of human life, no matter who is controlling it, is to love whoever is around to be loved.'" The maxim has special meaning to Salo, who, as a machine, pays love the highest tribute by emulating human nature. Once touched by friendship with Rumfoord, he wants more. On Tralfamadore there is no such relation as friendship.

Earth is the place for love. Salo, when his space ship is repaired, gives Constant a friendly lift back to Earth. Constant returns not to wacky Hollywood, where he lived, or to stately Newport, where the novel begins, but to Indianapolis (which is Home Sweet Home for Vonnegut) because it was the first American locality in which a white man was hanged for killing an Indian. Beginning in Newport, swinging around space, concluding in Indianapolis, *The Sirens of Titan* counterbalances borrowed elegance with the homespun, the mansion with a two-story frame house, hierarchical privilege with everyday fairness. This dramatic change is the rhythm of justice. As for Constant, this weary traveler made it through the thick and thin of planet-hopping but dies waiting in the snow for a bus, the commuter's nightmare come true. Nevertheless, his life "would end well," the parabolist promises us; and it does. Salo hypnotizes Constant so that he will die with a golden dream of going off with Stony in a diamond-studded space ship to Paradise. Constant fulfills his destiny as an Earthling with the restoration of friendship. The blatant hallucinosis of Constant's reverie bids farewell to the actual world and reminds us of the fictiveness of this fiction. Earth greets him with "the wet kisses of snowflakes" composing a now "perfectly white world." What a way to go! We are put in mind of the western movie finale in which the hero moves on, into the sunset, alone, but with the memory of his lost friend, all of which is backed by plaintive music bringing us to "The End."

The requirements of the sentimental adventure story are more than amply fulfilled in *The Sirens of Titan*. When the novel concludes, the world is brought into precise focus as things come into a harmonious whole. It is no longer the junkyard it once was. That debris-ridden world is gone. In the end our perception of the world is corrected because Constant's perceptions have been made new through his space pilgrimage. The perfect white world at the conclusion depicts the world as though seen through Constant's moral freshness. He has come to see—we have come to see in the act of reading his parable—that our humanity is forever present, not something to be pursued or awaited, but only to be perceived and realized by loving whoever is around to be loved, as we sail together on this planet through the cold blue.

3

MOTHER NIGHT

> Through the years, a man peoples a space with
> images of provinces, kingdoms, mountains,
> bays, ships, islands, fishes, rooms, tools, stars,
> horses, and people. Shortly before his death,
> he discovers that the patient labyrinth of lines
> traces the image of his own face.
> Jorge Luis Borges, *A Personal Anthology*

Howard W. Campbell, Jr. is the central figure in *Mother Night* (1961),
Vonnegut's third novel. Campbell is a writer, a playwright to be more
precise, who was born on February 16, 1912, in Schenectady, New York,
where his father, like the Iliumites of *Player Piano,* devoted his talent to
making better electrical products for better living. Foster-child of industry,
he is taken to Berlin in 1923 at the age of eleven, when his father is
transferred to the firm's branch there. Though his parents return at the
outbreak of World War II in 1939, Howard, Jr. stays on to make a life
for himself as a writer in Germany. Feeling exempt from the war because
of his artistic calling, he refuses to take a moral stand. War, however, especially one precipitated by the more than usually savage aims of Nazism,
demands a decisive moral response. Campbell hedges. Though he sees the
corruption around him, he wants to pursue his career in Germany. So he
assuages his conscience by being loyal to America. His double allegiance
creates the conflict of his life, which is the drama of the novel, another
tale from the fabled lunacy of Weimar-Third Reich Berlin.

Campbell becomes a double agent. Major Frank Wirtanen enlists him as
an American undercover spy. The cover is that of a broadcaster extolling

the virtues of fascism to the English-speaking world and attacking the Allies. Espionage seems just right to Campbell. He can earn a living when times have put people in peaceful trades out of work; he can serve the forces of good; and above all, he can indulge his instinct to be a ham and "fool everyone with my brilliant interpretation of a Nazi." Campbell becomes another of Vonnegut's unwitting human relays in an incomprehensible communications network. As the Earthlings in *The Sirens of Titan* pass on messages that they are unaware of transmitting, Campbell sends out in his broadcasts coded information that he knows nothing about. His attempts to control the meaning of his speeches enmesh him further in duplicity. He tries to be satiric by taking Nazi propaganda to an extreme, but the world is so wacky that hyperbole comes off as a modest proposal. When he presents the rantings of a wild anti-Semite to expose the crudity and ludicrousness of anti-Semitism, his listeners take him seriously. Campbell is at the mercy of his grimly stupid audience. We have met this anonymous group of dupes before in Vonnegut's fiction. In *Player Piano* they rallied at the Meadows to worship the technology that was doing them in. They assembled again in *The Sirens of Titan* for Rumfoord's annunciation of The Church of God of the Utterly Indifferent. They constitute in *Mother Night* an international band eager to hate, ready to believe the racist dogma Campbell is mouthing. Soon Campbell has a life to go with his pretense. He struts around Nazi circles "like Hitler's right-hand man, and nobody saw the honest me I hid so deep inside."

If someone had seen that true self, Campbell would have been spared pain and harassment. As events turn out, when the war is over, Campbell is hunted down as a Nazi war criminal. Until 1960 he lives in relative seclusion in New York City. Then further intrigue exposes him. Cries for punishment arise around the world, and reach Campbell's conscience. He turns himself in to the Israeli government for prosecution. Just one day before the actual trial, Wirtanen sends a letter explaining that Campbell worked for America during the war. Freed through Wirtanen's intervention, Campbell decides to hang himself "for crimes against himself."

All of this action occurs before the novel begins. The drama proper covers no physical action at all. *Mother Night* takes place in jail, opening with Campbell behind bars in Jerusalem and concluding with him locked up in the same place, about to commit suicide. The bare facts of time and place, along with the polarities of its dramatic movement, say a great deal about the growth of Vonnegut's work, and we may pause briefly to note his development. Strife, brutality, spiritual loss—these and other themes from the first two books recur in *Mother Night;* but now the treatment of such issues is more personal, more psychological. It takes place in the present, not in the future. The setting shifts accordingly from the outer space of *The Sirens of Titan* to inner space. The story unfolds not by flinging out through celestial bodies but by burrowing down into psychic places within a single person. Having ventured into the cosmos, Vonnegut for this adventure confines himself to the microcosm of the self. The exploration of this inner galaxy is best made through introspection rather than the mock-utopian or parable treatments of the earlier novels. Such a book might very well have been expected, though its story could not have been predicted. Near the beginning of *The Sirens of Titan*, the narrator declares that "Only inwardness remained to be explored." Campbell's confession gives shape to that remaining exploration. Finally, we can say this about the thematic contours of Vonnegut's first three novels: if *Player Piano* affirms the growth of the individual through revolt, and if *The Sirens of Titan* goes on to show a positive, miraculous conversion of the self, *Mother Night* redirects the moral energy by dramatizing a negative artistic conversion. Campbell turns out to be what he pretended to be. His mask of Nazi propagandist becomes his personality. By mutilating language, Campbell subverted his talent into an instrument of evil. In his own lamenting words, "The artist in me got turned into ugliness such as the world has rarely seen before."

Several critics have recognized that Vonnegut is after something new in *Mother Night*, and they have praised his achieving of it. Robert Scholes says in a recorded conversation with Vonnegut, "The book of yours that seems a little bit different from all the others, and I think perhaps my favorite of them all, is *Mother Night*. It seems a little darker than the others, a little less comic, but by no means a satire."[1] The exchange took place in 1966, at the University of Iowa, so Scholes has in mind all of the fiction up to *Slaughterhouse-Five* (1969). Vonnegut himself was quick to agree with Scholes that *Mother Night* has a special place in his work. "It's more personally disturbing to me," he admits. "It had meanings for me. Oh, because of the war and because of my German background, and that sort of thing."[2] Looking at the novel from the standpoint of technique, Ihab Hassan in 1972 finds *Mother Night* to be "Vonnegut's most complex work."[3] Actually, there is little need to rehearse the favorable reception of *Mother Night;* Jerome Klinkowitz capsulizes it for us in his 1973 survey of Vonnegut's artistic development when he observes that "many critics today call [*Mother Night*] his best" work.[4]

II

Three points have been made here about *Mother Night*. In recounting its story, I called attention to the distinctive approach to the novelist's standing theme of selfhood. The inward focus of the technique, I then suggested, extends certain moral directions that were proposed but not pursued in *Player Piano* and *The Sirens of Titan*. Critical regard for *Mother Night* indicates recognition of the new power of the novel by implicitly placing it as a watershed in the development of Vonnegut's career. The observations, of course, are of a piece. What is called for now is a demonstration of that interrelation, a consideration of how Vonnegut makes something new by taking up an old subject to move forward.

A particularly apt way into the complexity of *Mother Night* is through form. This confessional story requires of the reader a certain literary sophistication, for the book is, after all, told by a literary artist revealing his abuses of literary forms. Tony Tanner, who reads contemporary fiction astutely, has noticed that *Mother Night* "presents, almost in shorthand, a whole spectrum of fiction-making, from the vilest propaganda to the most idealistic art."[5] This display of various kinds of inventions is one aspect of Vonnegut's making form the subject of his novel. Another aspect comes through Campbell's direct comments on language, which ironically yield his best insights into his behavior. Art can do this. In Campbell's case it must because his absorption into this self-created Nazi monster equates the crisis of his life with the task of his art. But I am running a bit ahead of the argument here. With an abstract problem such as form, it is best to get down to cases immediately.

It is an indication of how bemused Campbell is that he should broadcast the news of his wife Helga's death without knowing it. When Wirtanen tells him about the coded death notice, Campbell says nothing about the woman he loved and promptly overcomes his anger at being used shamelessly; but at the time he does grieve over missing the occasion to destroy himself properly. Suicide for Campbell is a matter of aesthetics. Theoretically, his beloved's death is a cue to take his own life. The effect would create the perfect symmetry of form called for by heroic drama. We know the formula—Isolde eagerly takes the love-potion to follow

Tristan to transcendent splendor. In Wagner's version the playing of the violins upon our hearts says that it cannot be otherwise. Does Juliet hesitate to stab herself when she finds her true love poisoned? Their *Liebestod* culminates everything preceding it. The lovers are absorbed into an ecstasy that leaves nothing unfulfilled. Campbell wants his life to imitate that genre. Missing Helga is one thing, but missing his chance " 'for the great suicide scene' " is grave. His deepest passion belongs to his sense of form. "'I admire form,'" he pronounces to Wirtanen. "'I admire things with a beginning, a middle, an end—and, whenever possible, a moral, too.'"

The dramatic pattern that he admires would have a clear exposition of the characters that leads into complication of the characters' problems, which would be tied together in the resolution. In such a pattern the ending, which is where the materials of a work are fully realized, leaves little or nothing for the reader to wonder about. Campbell admires the kind of ending that closes off the whole, a pattern we readily recognize. Children's stories and fairy tales usually leave us with a sense of the characters living happily ever after. Biblical parables neatly conclude to make the instruction unmistakable. The design can be complex, as in Greek tragedy, which carries its dramatic energy to a high degree of finality to express the force of fate. It is useful to recall these instances because the structure of art implies a structure of the world; and where a story follows a logical or causal development, it expresses a correspondingly coherent world—looked over by God, say, or ruled by Fate. So Campbell's preference for form contains an entire aesthetic of literature and view of experience.

Campbell's personal history should have taught him that there are *forms* and that a work has *a* form, but *the* form does not exist except as an ideal or textbook exercise. A pattern based on clarity and causality could not accommodate his own life, which is a series of disconnections. But Campbell's fate is not to know all that he is communicating. While he states a preference for ideal form, his achieved form in his confessions is highly individual. The novel itself renders the shape of his experience. Chapter One appears to initiate the tale with a classical introduction of the main character and his dilemma.

My name is Howard W. Campbell, Jr.
    I am an American by birth, a Nazi by reputation, and a nationless person by inclination.
    The year in which I write this book is 1961.
    . . . .

I am behind bars.
I am behind bars in a nice new jail in old Jerusalem.
I am awaiting a fair trial for my war crimes by the Republic of Israel.

The beginning establishes the fictive world of *Mother Night* as that of Campbell's mind. The rhetoric reveals a crisis. The litany of facts and repetitious syntax are part of Campbell's bafflement. Emotionally, he is stuck; the string of loose sentences cannot go forward. He is blocked in a cell of words; hence the physical jail. Setting and mind become interchangeable. The terms of his imprisonment further alter our sense of the beginning of the novel. He is awaiting trial and, as things stand, certain execution by the Israeli government. The beginning of his memoir is really a crisis. The man who commends stories with a definite beginning starts his own memoir well past the middle of his life, very near the end. Vonnegut's formal irony here tells us more about Campbell than does his aesthetic manifesto. Vonnegut uses a form of dislocation. This "citizen of nowhere" tells his story in a halting rhetoric of anxiety over his destruction. We have, I would say, a hanging beginning.

Chapter One may strike the note of a beginning, but it is not the book's formal beginning. *Mother Night* has more than its usual share of front matter and antecedent paraphernalia: an Introduction that was added in 1966 when the book was reissued in hardback, an Editor's Note from the 1961 original edition, the routine title page, a facetious dedication to Mata Hari (that is revised in the text by the mysterious Editor), and an epigraph from Sir Walter Scott. Ordinarily, we read and pass over such material. Taken individually, no one item seems striking. Here, however, Vonnegut ties the usually tangential matter to Campbell's recollection as part of a dialectic between book format and the story. We do not customarily regard the printed object before us as an organism, but Campbell's confession does take on life enough to generate these preliminaries. Each addition in the series pushes back the beginning of the action. Having played Editor in the 1961 edition, to establish a particular verisimilitude (he is polishing but not making up the text), Vonnegut steps out of that feigned posture in the Introduction to provide his personal experience with fascism in Indianapolis and with imprisonment as a soldier in Dresden. The reader's customary stance toward story has been changed for the reading of this book. We do not willingly suspend disbelief. The dividing line between life and fiction is erased. Can we imagine *Pride and Prejudice* opening up in this way without being malformed? *Mother Night* is re-formed by extension, the first sequence of which states:

This is the only story of mine whose moral I know. I don't think it's a marvelous moral; I simply happen to know what it is: We are what we pretend to be, so we must be careful about what we pretend to be.

Vonnegut, the actual artist, belatedly gives the moral that Howard W. Campbell, Jr., the fictive hero, has an inkling of but cannot come up with. The maxim holds that the imagination is an active moral force. By this light, art—progeny of the imagination—and life are one. Campbell's devolving into the Nazi image he concocted shows the truthfulness of the proposition. The interplay between the writing *about* the story and the writing *in* the story is Vonnegut's structural equivalent of Campbell's dilemma.

The beginning of *Mother Night* then, is really its multitude of beginnings. The fractured sequence serves a purpose. With each new start, the reader enacts Campbell's thwarted effort to get his personal investigation under way. The references in the beginnings become increasingly imaginative and allusive, gradually acclimatizing the reader to literary artifice as a mode of experience. The Editor warns of inaccuracies in Campbell's text and makes us even more wary by putting in a word for "lies told for the sake of artistic effect" because "in a higher sense" they can be "the most beguiling forms of truth." Then there is a lot of book-talk over name changes, spelling, italics, cuts, English versions, German versions, a discarded chapter, and a rededication that remains tucked in the Note. Vonnegut makes a good deal about seemingly extrinsic textual matter. We begin to sense that *Mother Night* is not only a book about life, which is the classical business of the novel, but also is a book that has living going on in its pages. Put another way, it shows life in form while using form to represent life. This of course is Campbell's problem stated anew. Campbell, like Don Quixote (after whom Chapter Thirty is titled and whose name he plans to adopt for an escape to Mexico City), would like to live in a literary text—high romance or a daring Mata Hari intrigue. He does so with fatal success.

It makes sense that Vonnegut's study of forms should take its title from yet another literary work. The title *Mother Night* is from Goethe's *Faust* and comes to the reader, as fits the preoccupation with books, replete with context and bibliographical data provided by the Editor. Mephistopheles introduces himself to Faust in the scholar's study (where else?) as the spirit of destruction competing against the new light to restore Mother Night, the first darkness, to her primordial rule. Here is the passage Vonnegut provides in the Editor's Note:

I am a part of the part that at first was all, part of the darkness that gave birth to light, that supercilious light which now disputes with Mother Night her ancient rank and space, and yet can not succeed; no matter how it struggles, it sticks to matter and can't get free. Light flows from substance, makes it beautiful; solids can check its path, so I hope it won't be long till light and the world's stuff are destroyed together.

I leave for another critic the rich parallel ambiguity in play and novel about whether good triumphs over evil, but two connections are worth establishing. Through such figures as the Director and the Poet and text-within-text, such as the Walpurgis Night's Dream, and direct speeches on art and life, Goethe shapes his drama with a keen consciousness of form. The very first line of Goethe's own belated Dedication is an apostrophe to form. "Again you come, you wavering forms!" His Faust, moreover, is the archetypal wanderer lost in the labyrinth of disorder and perplexity that surrounds Campbell and all of Vonnegut's other characters.

III

The labyrinth describes *Mother Night* perfectly. For Campbell the entire recollection of his attempt to serve truth, which actually did great harm, is an intellectual repetition leading to chaos. Goethe's words in his Dedication to *Faust* picture this confused mental place where "Grief is renewed, laments retrace the maze / of Life's strange labyrinthian career. . . ."

Mother Night is a lament that maps out two labyrinths. Campbell lives as a prisoner of his deceptions, which lead to further intricacies and, ultimately, to insanity. Life, then, is the first labyrinth. Here he dwells with "Hitler or Goebbels or Hoess or Goering or any of the other nightmare people of the world war numbered 'two.' " The repetition of the aimless syntactical "or" indicates his stumbling in the maze of language. Then, there are the convolutions of techniques. We saw the snagged beginnings. We will find overlayings of various narrative patterns which will show that art is the second labyrinth. Though Campbell, the child of Mother Night, is forever lost in the jumble, these cubicles of narration are available to the reader's overview.

Within the larger frame of the memoir, we see the sharp outline of the spy story initially told by Wirtanen when he enlists Campbell as a secret agent before the war in 1938. Wirtanen is sitting on a park bench (a standard tableau of intrigue) thinking up "'a pretty good spy story.'" The story he tells has Campbell as hero and foretells what will happen in Campbell's life, down to the United States' eventual refusal to confirm or deny his spying. Campbell steps from life into this spy script. Living out that story creates two other spy stories. The first is the novel itself, through which Campbell reexperiences Wirtanen's scheme without comprehending it. The second is an international subplot to get Campbell out of hiding in New York City to stand trial. In this story the characters are all double agents recognizable by their bizarre masks: the G-man; the beautiful one whose sexuality is her calling card (here it is Helga's younger sister Resi *playing* Helga to catch Campbell, whom she loves); the Black Fuehrer; the Reverend Dr. Lionel J. D. Jones, D. D. S., D. D., properly pedigreed for his supporting role in American fascism; Father Keeley, up from Skid Row to get commies; Kraft-Potapov, the Russian Master Spy; and assorted Patriots and innocent bystanders from Central Casting. And since a spy story is incomplete without a raid and a Luger, Vonnegut provides a raid and a Luger.

A classical spy story has the formulated design of beginning, middle, and end that Campbell likes. The plot exists for the solution. Any departure from this recipe violates the mental appreciation of the adventure because the spy story and its cousin the whodunit, are essentially abstract problems posed through a plot.[6] Can we imagine a James Bond story ending without the usual legal and sexual settlements? Vonnegut's interest in espionage lies elsewhere, however, since Campbell's career as a spy is all over at the beginning of the story, and the pursuers are clumsy and stupid. Their ineptitude makes it necessary for Campbell to turn himself in. Vonnegut clearly parodies the formal unity of the mystery story, leaving the reader one clue to his use of spying: Campbell's vocation. Vonnegut sees that crime and art can be comparable acts, as they are for Campbell, who lifted Nazi morale with his golden tongue. Sending concealed messages through people is also indictable as an abuse of language. (This case remains unsolved for we never get to the culpable agency behind the anonymous syndicate.) The presence of Adolf Eichmann in *Mother Night* puts the relationship of art to crime on a level of moral seriousness that makes Campbell's activity a misdemeanor. Eichmann steps out of history into fiction for a guest appearance in Tel Aviv, where Campbell passes through briefly while Eichmann is awaiting trial. "'I'm a writer now,'" Eichmann says. "'I never thought I'd be a writer.'" When writer-turned-Nazi meets Nazi-turned-writer, shoptalk is bound to follow. Eichmann speaks of language with the same deadly inability to recognize right from wrong that allowed him to hasten the slaughter of six million Jews. In his writing he attempts to justify Auschwitz. He is still a killer, now working his atrocity on words. And words, the novel has shown, can do great harm.

If the artist can be a criminal, we have to consider the possibility that a criminal can be a creative artist. The possibility does not tax the imagination. We frequently admire ingenuity, whatever the ethics. Certain crimes are so masterfully executed that the doers seem to deserve to win. Some criminals are too beautiful to lose. Marlene Dietrich behind bars is unthinkable, veneration makes more sense. Campbell entertains the idea of achieving recognition through finely turned radio satires of Nazi beliefs. Though he savors his own niceties of wit, such subtleties go over the heads of the countless Joneses and Keeleys of the world.

The bust scene brings the spy adventure to a grand finale, the kind of definite conclusion Campbell looks for in art. The cue for the end comes with the fascist Dr. Jones's salute to the colors as he is arrested. "'My only regret . . . is that I have but one life to give to my country.'" The boss G-man accepts Jones's regrets and assumes the role of director to clear the stage, as the script requires, "'Take it [the flag] away from him!'" So much for the patriotic cloak-and-dagger episode. But the novel continues, for the arrest of the spy ring leads the reader into the adjacent compartment of the labyrinth where a revenge drama is playing itself out.

Wirtanen gets Campbell freed from jail in the same secret way that he spared Campbell from facing charges after the war. When Campbell returns to his attic apartment in Greenwich Village, he finds the place in a shambles. Sitting on an overturned galvanized bucket waiting for him is Bernard B. O'Hare, who captured Campbell fifteen years ago in Germany and now is angry about the spy's freedom. Since learning of Campbell's seclusion in New York, O'Hare has been lying in wait for him; and he beats the Boston posse down to get him alone. He quotes himself, saying to strangers he met at a bar that day about his mission:

"I said to them, 'Sorry, boys—but this is a party just for Campbell and me. That's the way it's got to be—just the two of us, face to face,'" he said.

O'Hare reacts in strict accordance to the style of the grade-B western that has given him his male identity. "'You're pure evil. . . . You're absolutely pure evil.'" Schooled in the fantasy world of moral absolutes that divides the world into good guys and bad guys, O'Hare knows that corruption demands retaliation. Of course God is on his side. "'I'll show you, by God, I was born just to take you apart right here and now.'" In the fantasy fight, where he spends most of his life, O'Hare wins because good is supposed to win. But he's drunk and infirm and no match for Campbell's actual anger. Campbell perceives that O'Hare has allegorized his fury, has made himself St. George slaying the dragon. This dragon, Campbell, however, has been in a number of other legends, some of which he wrote with himself as victor. Bad guy or evil spirit, Campbell does not want to be a minor character in the play O'Hare has fantasized, so Campbell breaks the would-be avenger's right arm with firetongs and shoves him onto the landing. The revenge drama ends not with moral forces rectified, but in a mess, and with an image of that free-floating hatred that gives many characters in the book their reason for existing. O'Hare throws up, then runs off physically battered but morally undiminished in his compulsive proclamation of himself through malevolence. "'I'll get you yet, brother.'" One of Mother Night's brats runs off spitefully. Another closing of another show.

Campbell objects, not to being assigned a role, but to being assigned that particular one in a piece with O'Hare as star. Campbell would willingly be the male lead in a romance. He wrote a play called *Das Reich der Zwei*, or *Nation of Two*, which captures the life he desires: he and his lovely wife Helga are the nation of two; their great double bed is their territory. Their pact to love secures them against the brutal actual world, and on their lovers' Noah's Ark they can survive the flood of violent madness that is inundating the world. *Das Reich der Zwei* unites Campbell's truest loyalties, art and love. The real world, however, has a way of shattering the ideal retreats we construct in fancy. Helga was captured by the Russians when she was entertaining the troops in the Crimea, and she died in exile from the nation of two. Her death, and his failure to kill himself according to the treaty of romance, raze their lofty kingdom. "And when that nation ceased to be, I became what I am today and what I always will be, a stateless person." The love story he wants to inhabit also fails to complete itself.

But the memoir of Howard W. Campbell, Jr. goes on; and it does so by incorporating each of the fractured literary forms that shapes his life. This more capacious totality of his confessions has no clear beginning, as we saw; nor has it a middle as readers expect a middle. Instead of an even unfolding of related events we have a series of endings of stories within the confession that string out like sporadic anticlimaxes. I have explored three such set pieces—the spy story, the revenge drama, and the romance. There are others, namely, an "allegory in the Victorian manner," the legend of the Holy Grail, and the marvelous history of Campbell's manuscripts, which live on as imaginary beings and even give new life to one Stepan Bodovskov, the Russian corporal, who translates Campbell's plays and becomes their author. Other readers will certainly detect other parodies. These discoverable forms, along with those brought to light here, collectively suggest an infinity of connections of person within person and place within place in the manner of Jorge Luis Borges. For Campbell these links are treacherous. Each substory turns a door into a wall in the labyrinth of his mind as he tries to get to the center of himself. He cannot enter the meaning of his life by extracting form from form, taking off mask after mask. The total effect of this endless convergence is an erasing of the margin between art and life. Vonnegut's achieved form, I would say, observes the fantastic unity that he spoke of in the Introduction, between what we imagine ourselves to be and what we become.

The ending of *Mother Night* compresses the diffuse energies of Campbell's meditation into one anti-event. Freed by Wirtanen's help, he holds court on himself and decides to commit suicide, a choice which Vonnegut handles with special moral acuteness. When the British liberated the concentration camp at Belsen in 1945, they compelled the guards to bury their victims in mass graves. Campbell performs the same retributive service and faces his crimes by interring the multiple pretender selves he abused. The turncoat writer has stood a prisoner of his own image all along, so the moral sentence follows from the solipsistic world Campbell inhabits. This gesture too remains painfully incomplete. Though he proclaims his impending self-destruction, the novel leaves the reader with the sense that Campbell does not follow through with his announcement. We are left with the split response that is at the center of his personality. With characteristic dramatic flourish he bids, "Goodbye, cruel world!" Then, with an equally typical about-face, he speaks from another of his selves (now his dark, comic self) and follows his adieu with a histrionic gesture that raises the possibility that we will meet again—*"Auf wiedersehen?"* These words close the novel with the gallows humor that surrounds Vonnegut's stories. Moreover, by concluding the memoir with a question mark, Vonnegut suspends Campbell's self-examination in an unfinished state. Like Dante's damned, Campbell is doomed emotionally to relive his crime without ever coming to a releasing understanding. So it does seem likely, as he says, that we will meet his many selves again and again. Campbell can never go beyond the minimal awareness of "my endless game," which amounts to encounters with disguise after disguise.

Vonnegut is making a moral point through the ambiguous ending of *Mother Night.* The scripts Campbell tries to live by are inadequate to the contingencies of life. The pain caused by remorse is awful, but worse pain comes from the recognition that there is no resolution. Early in the novel Campbell speaks of "'something worse than Hell'" to his Israeli prison guard. Hell is decisive next to the purgatorial rotation of pretenses that leads nowhere. We have a hung ending to parallel the hung beginning. Rhetorical gesture serves as moral retribution. Campbell's imminent suicide is a comment on the world he lives in as well as on his personal despair; only in a nihilistic world could the gratuitous taking of one's life be a way of affirming oneself, as it is for Campbell. Mother Night is in the throes of giving birth to another dark child of despondence.

The ironies of the ending remind the reader to view the maze wholly from the outside and invite us to exercise our moral imagination to piece together the confusion that destroys the protagonist. This is the responsibility ironic art such as Vonnegut's places on the reader. From the outside a pattern does suggest itself. In trying to comprehend his heartsickness and penitence, Campbell moves from an egocentric view of his personal importance (he will dazzle the world with his brilliant speeches) to a recognition of his personal insignificance. "'Nobody even knows I'm alive anymore.'" Doomed and with his fantasy defenses down, Campbell confronts the idea of his personal extinction. His ego, which was once so grandiose that it hatched many make-believe selves to secure endurance, now is presented with the fact of its noncontinuance. The mind encounters no greater difficulty than realizing its nonexistence. Campbell deals with this intolerable dilemma with the same subterfuge he used to handle other dangers. Now he thinks of himself as dead, but his idea of suicide wrests only illusory power over impending doom. *Mother Night* lays bare for us the mechanism of the self-deceiving mind as it desperately tries to keep up with the uncontrollable distresses of life, which, for Vonnegut, are epitomized in the encompassing threat of war with its senseless violence.

What is predicated of suffering at the hands of one's enemies is actually a form of presentation of the human self to be embraced by another. Campbell's revelation of his progressive abandonment impresses on our minds the consoling necessity for love. One answer to the ego's seemingly unanswerable fear of extinction is its capacity to relate to other egos. "'What is life without friends?'" he asks Resi. In his exhausted voice we hear the underlying spirit of the novel expressing compassion for all the "gatherer[s] of wind-blown trash in the tracks of war." But Campbell can see no way of getting into life to live by the deepest truth of his self-investigation. The world for him remains a chimera. His suffering derives from sharing in its shadowiness. Having left the world a poorer and darker place for supporting tyranny, he inhabits a desolation of his own making.

4

CAT'S CRADLE

> I think the Commonwealth of Learning is
> chiefly obliged to the great *Modern* Improve-
> ment of *Digressions*. . . .
> Jonathan Swift, *A Tale of a Tub*

The story of *Cat's Cradle* is told by a free-lance writer called, quite simply, John, whose recent project is a book about the day Hiroshima was bombed—August 6, 1945—to which he has given the working title *The Day the World Ended*. In order to get background material, John decides to research the private life of Dr. Felix Hoenikker who was, in the grim familialism we have adopted toward our nuclear progeny, one of the fathers of the atomic bomb. Gathering details about Hoenikker involves John with the man's three children, whose lives lead John through a chain of events culminating in a disaster surpassing the Hiroshima calamity he intended to write about. John never does get back to his original subject. The Hoenikker side of the project drifts, or literally digresses, from the main issue and takes on a narrative importance of its own until the Hiroshima material disappears and the digression becomes the novel.

Cat's Cradle, then, is a digression about the Hoenikker family, and this displacement of the narrator's proclaimed topic by a subsidiary one alerts us to Vonnegut's intention in his fourth novel. His meaning lies precisely in the book's narrative detour; for swerving reflects Dr. Hoenikker's devia-tion from responsibility in his scientific research, a deviation which brought about the Hiroshima disaster in the first place and then yielded *ice-nine*, which finally destroys the entire world.

John survives to tell about the later calamity and changes his name to one more in keeping with trial he has endured. "Call me Jonah," are his first words. His phraseology pointedly aligns Vonnegut's narrator with Melville's storyteller Ishmael in *Moby Dick*, and by extension with the classical American artists who are, as William Carlos Williams terms them in *Paterson*, "Ishmaels of the spirit." Having narrowly escaped in their pursuit of the great white whale of knowledge, such people survive to tell us of the world's incomprehensibility. The spirit of Ishmael is that of prophecy born of affliction. Vonnegut makes of his spiritual Ishmael a darker figure who shadows forth the dire warning that we must change our ways if we are to avoid universal annihilation. The bearer of cosmic news is as familiar a figure in Vonnegut's books as is the conflict between "know-how" and "know-what." The threat of technological advancement without regard for ethical purpose necessitates the omens issued by the messenger. By placing the pursuit of knowledge in the atomic age under the sign of Jonah, Vonnegut in *Cat's Cradle* has extended the responsibility of the envoy and, therefore, the character of his news. The Old Testament context brought into play through Jonah warrants our attention because it provides guidelines for understanding Vonnegut's artistry.

The little Book of Jonah is an anomaly among the prophetic books of Israel. It foregoes the customary collection of oracles in favor of humor to convey God's word; its artistry is matchless in prophetic literature. The story of Jonah is a comic novella about a prophet who hardly fits the traditional picture of those disturbing men whose voices rock the world. Prophets usually cry out God's word with brave disregard of consequences; but when God commands Jonah to go to Nineveh to announce his intention to destroy the city for its wickedness, Jonah hops a ship to Tarshish, which lies in the opposite direction. God reacts to Jonah's evasion with a storm, imperiling the lives of all the sailors on the ship Jonah has boarded. They are saved only when Jonah is thrown into the sea, where, as we know even without reading the Old Testament, he is swallowed by a large fish in whose belly he spends three days and three nights. God rescues Jonah and orders him again to go to Nineveh. At this point in the narrative, after three distressful days in the belly of the fish, Jonah is back where he started. This time he obeys God and proclaims Nineveh's destruction with such power that the city repents. The people's turning away from evil moves God to spare Nineveh, meaning, of course, that Jonah's prophecy is not realized. In fact, God's change of plan dejects Jonah. He feels trapped. When he tries to avoid delivering the message, he is punished horribly; when he obeys, the message is negated and Jonah is made to appear foolish. His displeasure gives rise to the legitimate question of just how reliable God is. The Book of Jonah seems to answer that the Lord's word is not firm, that his anger is not absolute. Jonah cannot comprehend this ambiguity. He prefers to see Nineveh wiped out for the sake of his need for certitude. Besides, he rationalizes, he knew that God would be merciful and that is why he made haste to Tarshish. In light of this bafflement, Jonah prefers death to confusion. "I beseech thee," he says to God, "it is better for me to die than to live" (Jonah 4:3). God responds to Jonah's amusing self-righteousness and despair with a question: "And should not I pity Nineveh, that great city, in which there are more than a hundred and twenty thousand persons who do not know their right hand from their left, and also much cattle?" (Jonah 4:11).

God's question concludes the Book of Jonah, and strikes the crucial theological note of the text, emphasizing compassion for the repentant Nineveh over Jonah's desire for justice at any cost. Jonah values the completion of his task as God promised it over the continuance of human life. For God such consistency seems unimportant. God's pity for Nineveh effectively undermines any hope Jonah might have of finding a settled, predetermined order behind God's plan. God is free to change his word as he chooses without regard for what humans might have in mind about God's keeping his word. God does not even permit the prophet of his choice smugly to count on the infallibility of his word. In such a theology, clarity of purpose from the human perspective gives way to the splendid mystery of divine compássion. It is a theology of mystery.

From a résumé of the Book of Jonah and from a brief analysis of its meaning, we can see its appeal to Vonnegut's moral imagination. Comedy in the service of prophecy expresses the two modal energies of levity and gravity that he works through. Moreover, uniting comedy and prophecy enlarges our sense of both forms. Within the Jonah story, neither the events nor the story's large meaning moves in a straight line: Jonah's purpose comes about through digression; his obedience is arrogant; his success brings despair. But the theology of the Book of Jonah has an even deeper appeal to Vonnegut's sympathy. God's purpose is hidden behind contingency, which from the limited human view easily accommodates the absurdity of the universe. Here God incorporates the ambivalence experienced by the modern person at every moment. The Book of Jonah closes with a question from God, and that question leaves matters suspended in reflection rather than in dogma. Here is the God who shows us that deliverance—and not mere actualization—is the fulfillment of prophecy. The sign of Jonah is precisely such deliverance achieved through preaching. Vonnegut implies through his novelistic use of Jonah that science has led us so far astray that the enormous cry of Old Testament prophecy is needed to correct the course of life. *Cat's Cradle* is a sharp appeal for deliverance from the incursions of science, which Vonnegut before was satisfied merely to deride. As with its masterly ancient model, Vonnegut's little book of Jonah calls for special appreciation of the literary form in which its message is clothed.

The setting of Jonah's search marks the religious character of his mission. The pivotal events occur during Christmastide. There is "that fateful Christmas Eve" when Dr. Hoenikker dies—fateful because on that holy evening his three children received the direful gift of *ice-nine.* Their father's plaything, *ice-nine,* was all he had to give his children, and his last Christmas is the nativity of the world's end. Years later, Jonah begins his search during Christmas, and his experience shows how the hope once promised by the season has been overtaken by an unfolding doom. Meanwhile, the atomic bombing of Hiroshima has intervened, placing Hoenikker's idling on a different level of accountability.

This new Jonah does not sojourn in a fish's belly; instead, he is swallowed up by two social monsters. The first is the technocracy for which Hoenikker worked, the Research Lab of the General Forge and Foundry in Ilium, New York, Vonnegut's ubiquitous spawning ground for American industrial monstrosities. The information Jonah receives about Hoenikker from his associates is valueless because they neither knew him nor understood his work; but the way his colleagues live and, especially, how they speak define perfectly the way Hoenikker developed as a scientist. They speak in memos, using a fatuous and bland language that exposes an inability to make moral discriminations. When they do try to make judgments, they come up with slick public relations salutes to the company. The place is peopled by versions of the vacant Miss Pefko, who takes dictation as though the English they use were Ethiopic. Mechanical speech seems to be the only communication available to those who surrender their sovereignty to a corporate leviathan. The famous passage from Hobbes's *Leviathan* which Julian Castle cites late in the novel applies to Ilium. "'The truth was that life was as short and brutish and mean as ever.'" Jonah sinks into the world of materialistic absolutism where pure research is a cover for profiteering and militarism and where no one questions what is going on. It is an ugly place, for Jonah describes the city as blanketed by a motionless smog. Befouled and stagnant, Ilium's atmosphere is the climate of Hoenikker's mind: a moral vacuum.

When Dr. Asa Breed, who runs the lab, boasts to Jonah that "'new knowledge is the most valuable commodity on earth,'" he exposes the abuse by which science operates. It practices a reverse alchemy whereby truth is debased into gadget. *Ice-nine* epitomizes such an inversion of truth. The Marines wanted a way to get out of mud, and Hoenikker came up with a way to freeze liquids at higher temperatures than usual. *Ice-nine* allows the Marines to suspend the law of nature and to play God by walking on water. "*Ice-nine* was the last gift Felix Hoenikker created for mankind before going to his just reward."

As Jonah goes deeper into this social beast, he sees that the absence of morality in the lab extended into Hoenikker's family life, where there was authority without feeling. His three children led loveless lives. Newt, the youngest, writes tenderly of his father's efforts to play with his small son; but the recollection reveals the pathos of the child's single contact with his father, for Dr. Hoenikker never played with Newt, and "'he had hardly ever even spoken to me.'" Franklin, or Frank, the older son, had almost "no experience in talking to anyone" as a child. The horse-faced daughter Angela was obliged to be mother to her brothers and servant to her father when Hoenikker's wife died from lack of love at Newt's birth. The physical appearance of Hoenikker's offspring displays the destruction their father fostered in the world: the midget Newt, the giantess Angela, the morbidly silent Frank. A Hoenikker family portrait blends the grisly elegance of a Charles Addams cartoon with the hideous exaggeration of *Mad* comics.

Not long after the Ilium expedition, Jonah gets caught up in the political deformity of San Lorenzo, a Caribbean island republic. San Lorenzo recalls its notorious namesake, Lorenzo the Magnificent of Florence, who exercised absolute authority tempered by appearances of republican equality. Lorenzo's dictatorship (from 1469 to 1492) taught Machiavelli a few things about political corruption. Vonnegut's mythical island bears a more immediate resemblance to Haiti under Papa Doc Duvalier, whose duplicity was less subtle than Lorenzo the Magnificent's, but equally despotic. When Jonah arrives on San Lorenzo, he finds that Franklin Hoenikker is serving as the Minister of Science and Progress—a political fact which confirms the inauspicious hints in the island's name.

San Lorenzo's highest mountain, Mount McCabe, is described in a way to indicate that Jonah-Ishmael is again meeting the elusive whale of unknowability. "It was a fearful hump, a blue whale, with one queer stone plug on its back for a peak. In scale with a whale, the plug might have been the stump of a snapped harpoon. . . ." The wounded leviathan is a defunct utopia where idealism has disintegrated into cynicism. In this banana republic without bananas, Jonah encounters tyranny, misery, deceit, and hopelessness. San Lorenzo is the earth stripped of its possibilities, for "God, in His Infinite Wisdom, had made the island worthless." Its history is the history of people's futile effort to correct God's wisdom. Lionel Boyd Johnson and Earl McCabe, who discovered the place, in 1922 (the year of Vonnegut's birth) set about applying their economic and legal skills to found a utopia. They fail. "Everybody was bound to fail, for San Lorenzo was as unproductive as an equal area in the Sahara or the Polar Icecap." It develops only by accident—one shipwreck brings the discoverers, yet another brings Frank, and Jonah himself "didn't feel that purposeful seas were wafting me to San Lorenzo." Born and sustained by chance, San Lorenzo is a terminus for human strays.

Where Ilium practices reverse alchemy, San Lorenzo engages in reverse theocracy. The state is governed by diabolic untruth. Johnson, whose name becomes Bokonon in the local dialect, establishes a religion to allow the inhabitants to endure their horrible life. Bokononism is a blatant opiate to blind people to the misery around them; and to ensure its success, McCabe and Bokonon forbid the practice of Bokononism and outlaw Bokonon himself, thereby giving the religion a kick and a scapegoat. Religion is but a distraction; good and bad are artificial distinctions concocted to oppress.

Jonah gradually becomes assimilated into San Lorenzo's corrupt politics and belief. The moment he arrives, Papa Monzano, the dictator, collapses in great pain and unexpectedly names Frank his successor; but Frank has no taste for rule and convinces Jonah to assume the presidency. Jonah agrees, mainly because marriage to the gorgeous Mona Monzano goes with the job. Mona is a debased Venus whose symbolic standing as a national shrine suggests Vonnegut's notion of politics as a derangement of sexual energies, which is the paradigm of the political order on San Lorenzo. Jonah's relationship with Mona is an expedient of power, unloving and entirely beyond the control of either party.

On San Lorenzo Jonah learns the process of victimship, or reverse selfhood. During his inauguration, when a plane crash brings the castle and Papa's frozen body into the sea (Papa had swallowed a vial of *ice-nine* to spare himself the misery of cancer), Jonah is engulfed by human bungling.

"I opened my eyes—and all the sea was *ice-nine*." He is trapped inside a glaciated planet, which is Vonnegut's version of Moby Dick's terrifying white blankness. He survives "the blue-white poison" physically by descending into an oubliette bomb shelter; and spiritually he lives with all he has been through by adopting the useful untruths of Bokononism. This Jonah emerges from the leviathan's interior to rail against human stupidity but not to promise deliverance from it. As a disciple of Bokonon, he tries to schematize a cynicism to cope with such omnipresent unthinking.

II

This account of Jonah's adventures shows how *Cat's Cradle* develops from the three novels preceding it. Resumed are the attacks on technology and the utopian aspiration registered in *Player Piano*. Where the managers run people's lives in the first book, in *Cat's Cradle* science wipes out the world; and where human efforts to set up a mechanized commonwealth resulted previously in an uprising against the synthetic community, they now harden into dictatorship. What holds the corrupt political order together on San Lorenzo is Bokononism, an elaborate version of the religious scheming in *The Sirens of Titan*. Rumfoord's Church of God of the Utterly Indifferent, however, is a benign pilot project in dealing with a godless universe next to the inquisitional cruelty of Bokononism. If the subjects come from the first two novels, the technique in *Cat's Cradle* derives from the third, *Mother Night*. Vonnegut's first-person narration makes *Cat's Cradle* a personal testimony to the warning of *Mother Night*, namely, that pretense and lies can overtake truth; for in *Cat's Cradle*, as Jonah tells his tale, lies systematically overtake actuality.

Critics have recognized the affinity among Vonnegut's first four novels; and seeing no advance in technique or change of theme, they tend to put *Cat's Cradle* aside. "Compared with the two preceding novels," Reed says, "it seems thinner in plot, more superficial and fragmentary in characterization, weaker in its ability to evoke emotion or concern, and consequently less substantial."[1] It is simply another of Vonnegut's parodies of the truths by which one lives, according to Max Schulz.[2] "The satire is there," Goldsmith allows, "but it is Horatian,"[3] by which he presumably means tame. With few exceptions, critical reaction has placed *Cat's Cradle* in Vonnegut's development as a résumé of what came before.

Repetition, however, can also refine meaning; and in observing the deepening of earlier interests in *Cat's Cradle,* we can see how this novel intensifies the attacks on politics and religion. This change in degree of treatment also makes for a change in kind of novel, and the kind of art Vonnegut aspires to in his fourth book is that of great satire.[4] *Cat's Cradle* belongs in the tradition of grand censure along with Swift's *A Tale of a Tub* and Blake's *The Marriage of Heaven and Hell.* Now, Swift and Blake are writers to whom Vonnegut admiringly alludes; and looked at by their lights, *Cat's Cradle* does shine, as Tanner says, as Vonnegut's "brilliant little fiction."[5]

Cat's Cradle shares in the mission of Swift's treatise and Blake's poem: all three show how the official teaching of religion is merely a rationalization toward the end of enduring a corrupt world and of gaining as much personal power as the venal world affords. For Swift the culprit is Christian Puritanism; for Blake, Swedenborgianism; for Vonnegut, the imaginary Bokononism, or any institutionalized belief. And in all three an intellectual corruption parallels the moral erosion. Swift takes on a gamut of learned fopperies that subvert truth. Blake goes after the false wisdom that artificially distinguishes between good and evil to subdue the human spirit. The intellectual abuse of our age for Vonnegut is science, which has gone beyond endangering the abstract ideal of truth to threaten everyday survival. When learning overcomes truth, it becomes sophistry; but when science overrides responsibility, it blasphemes life. These perils make it necessary to expose the "numerous and gross corruptions in Religion and Learning," as Swift phrases it, to protect humanity. The ugly images of the human form pervading *Cat's Cradle,* the *Tale,* and the *Marriage* embody the havoc already caused by these abuses. The body manifests soul; Swift's filth, Blake's tortured figures of contained energy, and Vonnegut's cartoon grotesques are the nauseating aspects of the human spirit calling for correction.

Blake will be valuable later in the discussion in understanding the apocalyptic ending of *Cat's Cradle.* For the total design of the novel, however, *A Tale of a Tub* offers an illuminating analogy. Two qualities of Swift's kind of satire bear on Vonnegut's strategy. In the *Tale,* Swift puts on a false mask and allows his Author to take on attitudes opposed to his own. This opposing figure permits Swift to work against his own fabrication. The disguise creates a parody of the attitudes it speaks for. A second technique enhances the first; the story of the *Tale* shows the Author imitating the very corrupt intellectual habits that he sets out to censure. Swift's skill in fashioning this ironic reenactment brings all the disparate parts of the treatise into an instructive whole. Disparateness is what the reader experiences in the *Tale,* and with disparateness the *Tale* progresses. The elaborate introductions, the double dedication, the self-conscious apologies and haughtiness, and above all the prodigious digressions *are* the form. In the *Tale* the reader is made to see that formlessness is a deliberate principle of design. The fragments collectively reveal how some human minds work. For Swift the mind goes by digression. By the time the *Tale* ends, digression overtakes the story (which incidentally is about three brothers), and robs the story of any dramatic impact by reducing it to insignificance.[6] Swift's assault on the form of the *Tale* carries an attack on our intellectual assumptions. Human wisdom, for instance, pretends to arise through systematic thinking but actually unfolds from randomness. What we mean by Swiftian satire—which is the high-water mark of the genre—is making the subjects of ridicule into organizing principles of form.

Vonnegut proceeds in the same way in *Cat's Cradle.* Jonah is not a character in the customary sense so much as he is a mock author. He is not a narrator with a personality developed from inherent qualities, for his several names tell us that he is a reduction to narrative expedient. Whether he is John, as he once was, or "had been a Sam, I would have been a Jonah still" because the name evokes the disaster that determined his being. In the post-apocalyptic void all identity is adventitious. He stands a fool before forces that propel him from project to project, from place to place, monster to monster. He wants "to examine all strong hints as to what on Earth we, collectively, have been up to" and rightly regards himself as more qualified "to answer those tough questions than any other human being," and yet he acknowledges that he can only rephrase the jumbled questions he raises. Though Jonah says that "nihilism was not for me," he becomes its unwitting spokesman. For all his unique experience teaches him, Jonah's life remains "meaningless." He tries to believe that love will make sense amid vast disorder and resigns himself to a loveless universe. "And no love waiting for me anywhere. . . ." Passive resignation allows Jonah to live in the failen world but it also allows him to be absorbed by the cynicism that destroyed the world. By becoming a Bokononist after his trip to San Lorenzo, Jonah rationalizes all that is irrational and doctrinizes irresponsibility; for the business of Bokononism, Julian Castle explains to Jonah (using language reminiscent of the Works's slogan in *Player Piano*) is "'to provide the people with better and better lies,'" to keep them from the truth, which is "'that life was as short and brutish and mean as ever.'"

Through its sustained digressions the novel follows Jonah's ineluctable reduction to the hopelessness he seeks to transcend. Beneath the surface event we can read the history of modern science and religion shifting from their original purpose—to provide knowledge and faith—to their harmful effects of destruction and deception. Vonnegut, however, writes more than allegory; he provides an account of Jonah's personal encounter with the false claims of science and religion—or to stay with the Old Testament myth, an account of his two ordeals within the modern leviathans. This frame gives Vonnegut the opportunity to study Jonah's individual vulnerability to the abuses that he is studying for hints about the meaning of life.

While the planet Earth in the novel falls apart completely, Jonah's world divides neatly into two parts. (The Book of Jonah is designed in halves—Jonah on the ship and at Nineveh.) Ilium and San Lorenzo fabulize the novel's double subject. One is the city of science; the other, the island of belief. Though each arises out of a separate intellectual system, they are twin states of being. Both have a facade of harmony that obscures a hideous life. Ilium's affluence compensates for its spiritual poverty; San Lorenzo proffers spirituality to fill its material want. Together they school Jonah in the futility of aspiring to improve or even to understand the human condition. Ilium presents him with the proudest achievement of the modern century, science, which finally is nothing more than the tinkerings of a Nobel laureate in a moral vacuum. Then on San Lorenzo he learns that the loftiest of human intentions, philanthropy and political idealism, are rooted in power play. Each adventure leads Jonah to a discovery that reverses his thinking. These dramatic reversals state the condition of inversion that Vonnegut closes in on.

Though the two setbacks parallel each other, they show a change in Jonah. His recollection of Ilium is shaded by Bokononist detachment, so it is difficult to know Jonah's mental stance when beginning his investigation of Hoenikker. We do know that his aborted project was "'to emphasize the *human* rather than the *technical* side of the bomb,'" so he has only a limited fascination with science. In fact, his sardonic responses to the staff of the lab suggest a healthy skepticism about the pretensions of pure research. After Hiroshima he is not likely to be taken in by the mythology of scientific disinterestedness. But he does have expectations, however minimal, about human feeling, and he respects achievement. What he learns about Hoenikker would raise the eyebrows of a misanthrope, however. This Nobel physicist not only worked in a moral void; he lived in it. "'People weren't his specialty,'" explains Newt; and on this score everyone agrees. His wife died for lack of love and understanding. "'Family things, love things,'" not even living held value for Hoenikker. Only truth did. But just what truth means to a man who once asked, "'What is sin?'" defies understanding. The best Jonah can make of such inanity is a Swiftian exercise. As Swift dismisses his treatise on learning as "a tale of a tub," which readers of his day would know signifies a cock-and-bull story, Jonah entitles his study of modern science *Cat's Cradle* to mock the mind of the acclaimed Nobel laureate as a mechanism for heightening triviality. Making a cat's cradle with string and waving the tangles before his kids was Hoenikker's one pastime, driving Newt, for one, crazy while schooling him in nihilism. "'A cat's cradle is nothing but a bunch of X's between somebody's hands, and little kids look and look and look at all those X's. . . .'" When the tension holding the string in shape is relaxed, *"'No damn cat, and no damn cradle,'"* complains Newt. The string game suggests to Jonah that truth for Hoenikker is a mere fabrication, a game, a whimsy momentarily poised over nothing. When he sees Newt's painting of a cat's cradle he wonders if the lines "might not be the sticky nets of human futility hung up on a moonless night to dry." Jonah's descent into the belly of Ilium shows him that the human side of the bomb is an emotional abyss, but Jonah's detachment allows him to handle this discouraging revelation.

Before descending into San Lorenzo, Jonah's capacity to resist a fatally negative view of the world is severely tested. He returns to his New York apartment from Ilium to find that a poet acquaintance named Krebbs left everything "wrecked by a nihilistic debauch." He burned the couch and killed Jonah's avocado tree and "sweet cat." Around the slaughtered cat's neck hangs a sign, "'Meow.'" It is the painful cry of a real cat treated as though it were the fake cat in the string game. The scene literalizes the abstract rules of the game. By literalizing language—a Swiftian master stroke—Vonnegut confronts Jonah with the nihilism implied in Hoenikker's leveling life down to idling. And Krebbs's pointless savagery momentarily dissuades Jonah from surrendering to the ethical anarchism he has been drawn to by the horrors he witnesses. Bokonon has a word for this event, as he has for everything: Krebbs is a *wrang-wrang* or "a person who steers people away from a line of speculation by reducing that line, with the example of the *wrang-wrang's* own life, to an absurdity."

San Lorenzo tests Jonah's turning away from nihilism. The island's abject misery would challenge the faith of a blind optimist; for Jonah, whose affirmation is tentative, the voyage is an insuperable ordeal. The irresponsibility of Ilium would be a luxury on San Lorenzo since there is nothing here to be irresponsible about. Everyone has thrown up his or her hands in despair. Questions of conscience that are raised about Ilium are beside the point of life on San Lorenzo because conscience implies moral choice, which is rendered nugatory by the people's having nothing to choose. "'Nobody objects to anything,'" Frank Hoenikker says. "'They aren't interested. They don't care.'" Even power, the cynic's protection, seems undesirable, and is unwanted, at any rate by Frank. His unprincipled refusal of San Lorenzo's rulership traps Jonah in the island's affairs. Like father, like son; authority entails the very duty that Frank cannot accept. The difference between the two episodes of moral renunciation is that with the son's, Jonah becomes implicated by agreeing to govern the forsaken island society. His motives are mixed with his sexual desire for Mona, to be sure; but Jonah still feels that he can improve the quality of life on San Lorenzo. His rising moral responsiveness is set against the refusals of moral accountability by the Hoenikkers.

Two strategies shape Jonah's San Lorenzo voyage: reduction and inversion. Their significance is most apparent in the series of ceremonies that unify the San Lorenzo adventure. The first ceremony is a rite of protocol for the new arrivals, among whom is the new American Ambassador, Horlick Minton. Formality requires that Papa Monzano himself greet the emissary. When Papa climbs from his Cadillac, the emaciated, rickety natives strike up the national anthem proclaiming that they are "Where the living is grand" to the tune of "Home on the Range." The anonymous Homesteaders of *Player Piano,* who became Rumfoord's motley believers in *The Sirens of Titan* and Campbell's duped listeners in *Mother Night,* reappear in malignant form. They are living repudiations of the anthem they utter and of the island's governance, which their agony exposes as self-aggrandizement. The welcome is really a repulsion, which is the appropriate greeting for this isle of alienation. The observance salutes deception. But the pain that seizes Papa during the entertainment marks the limit of people's vast powers of fabrication. ("When you're dead you're dead," reads the Introduction to *Mother Night.*) Papa's final decree of willing the presidency to Frank turns the proceedings into an investiture. Within the day Frank turns his ascendancy into an abdication—casting aside political power as he squandered the chemical power of *ice-nine.* Appalled by the populace's plight, Jonah is shocked and angered by Frank's turning away "from all human affairs."

The day after Jonah's arrival is The Day of the Hundred Martyrs to Democracy, the national holiday in honor of San Lorenzo's negligible contribution to World War II. That the martyrs were conscripted and immediately killed by a German submarine just outside the island's harbor does not matter. On San Lorenzo the botch is honorable because failure is all the islanders have. The actual celebration involves several rituals— the military memorial service, the engagement of Frank to the stunning Mona, who goes with the office of the presidency, to which is added the proclamation of Jonah as president after the wreath ceremony and the air show. There is a great deal of holiday-making but no pleasure. These ceremonies do not reset the stage of human life to give dignity and mystery. They are macabre dramas that shuffle the pawns around clumsily to trivialize their conduct and to impoverish them anew.

Jonah's inaugural reflections show how he is drawn more deeply into the deceptions he seeks to escape. At first, he thinks of having "the awful hook," which is used to kill people for rejecting Bokononism, removed; but then he realizes that he has nothing to put in its place to keep order through fear. Jonah acquiesces in despair because circumstances are too hopeless. His defeatism is more benign in tone than Krebbs's defilement, yet is finally just as culpable. Vonnegut tips the reader off to Jonah's moral hardening through his mounting egoism. "So I put my speech in my pocket and I mounted the spiral staircase in my tower. I arrived at the uppermost battlement of my castle, and I looked out at my guests, my servants, my cliff, and my lukewarm sea." His becoming boss does seem to be "my apotheosis," as Jonah revealingly calls it; and as a god he will be exempt from the human misery he is incapable of alleviating.

Rhetoric begins the inauguration but cataclysm ends it. Again, Vonnegut reduces words to fact. After the flatulent greetings from the American ambassador, the air raid sets off the explosion that brings Papa's *ice-nined* body cascading into the sea. This is not a memorial to the one hundred martyrs to democracy but the very martyrizing of humanity to tyrannical stupidity. All but a few perish—consumed in the belly of the whale. "My lukewarm sea had swallowed all." The whale again defies its hunters. Doomsday aptly commemorates life in this void in the Caribbean. That this sweltering tropical nowhere should freeze over into the gulping whale-like monster is right because ice epitomizes the emotional coldness that allowed Dr. Hoenikker to invent *ice-nine* and then selfishly to barter it, as Frank does to Papa for personal gain and as Angela does for a husband. In novel after novel, Vonnegut warns of the intellect's potential destructive power, showing us how its discoveries can prompt a person to try to rule over life, and death, and nature as would God. The world locked in ice depicts creation captive to arrogant intellectual error. The image looms satiric yet prophetic, insisting that we take this outcome into moral account while it entreats for the liberating heat of wisdom and the creative fire of the imagination to thaw creation back to life.

III

The day the world ends is also a day of betrothal in the novel. Frank's marriage to Mona Monzano is to be announced. This is nullified when Frank refuses to accept the presidency and asks Jonah to be president. Jonah agrees and gets the hand of Mona who, as "the national treasure," goes with the presidency. The unexpected juxtaposition of these bizarre nuptials and doomsday is part of Vonnegut's aim for grand satire.

In the Bible the end of the world is often compared to a wedding to symbolize the lasting union of humanity with the universe. *The Revelation of John* foretells the relation of the soul and the church to Jesus as that of bride and bridegroom. Blake in *The Marriage of Heaven and Hell* prefigures the oncoming world as the marriage of desire with cosmic light and heat. In Blake's scheme, when fiery human passions subsume the restraints of prudence, the God within us is released. The apocalypse, then, has a creative aspect since it brings about a lasting transformation of the momentary into the eternal. And so the wedding.

Vonnegut's apocalypse does not anticipate transcendence in this way. One engagement is nullified and the other, with Jonah, aborted by Mona's suicidal kissing of *ice-nine*, her true, demonic groom. The novel's ending fulfills these negations with a divorce of life from the earth by *ice-nine*, which holds the world in abiding irrelation. A super-feverish boil of 114.4° Fahrenheit would melt the ice but we are left with no sense of potential restoration of the world's parts into a whole. Much of the novel's meaning is manifested in the image of divorce. In a disjoined world people exist in loneliness. Appropriately, then, Jonah's post-apocalyptic writing of the story expresses no interest at all in establishing human relationships. He accepts living in ultimate disespousal. All along the reader has sensed, in the made-up calypso jiving, that meaning has separated from the words we use, indicating that a new language is needed. The mind-reeling rapidity of the clipped chapters (127 chapters in 191 pages) registers the divorce of thought from feeling as the segments of the novel flow apart—never again to be joined in conventional printed narration in Vonnegut's subsequent books.

Cat's Cradle describes a hell divorced from its redemptive spouse, heaven. Blake's *Marriage* bears closely here. His poem shows that "there is a real hell in the human mind, and it achieves the physical form of dungeons, whips, racks and all the miserable panoply of fear."[7] Ilium has a prison and it is the lab's "cloister of cement block," but San Lorenzo is a total penal colony. Mug shots and fatal warnings greet arriving passengers at the airport. The state emblem is a huge iron hook on a beam between two telephone poles which keeps the decrepit citizenry in line. "It was low and black and cruel." There are torture chambers, too. Finally, there is the day-to-day torment of being alive on San Lorenzo. The oubliette under Papa's residence best expresses the life of the place. Here Jonah and Mona take refuge during the apocalypse while the others make it to a dungeon. In doing so, they descend into the very structure of the human mind of our age. Survival, like life, is an oubliation. These refugees from *ice-nine,* trapped in mental bondage, duplicate the dungeoning of creation above them. The double image of imprisonment above and below is Vonnegut's counterpart of "infinite Abyss" in the *Marriage.* The image signifies the torture of self-annihilation.

The last part of Blake's poem presents, as Harold Bloom puts it, "an emblem of the negation of vision."[8] Blake sees a Devil in a flame rising before an Angel who is seated on a cloud above. The Angel, outwitted in a moral argument, embraces the flames and emerges again as the prophet Elijah or Devil. The transformed Angel becomes Blake's friend. Together they read the Bible "in its infernal or diabolical sense," which they will pass on to the world if the world "behave well."

Cat's Cradle concludes with a comparable encounter between Jonah and a swami leading to a promised infernal text about life. Like Blake, Jonah at the End sees a visionary, Bokonon, who was something of a prophet and now, by calculated inversion, becomes an outlawed devil. He is not consumed in flames but is dying slowly of *ice-nine.* Jonah and Bokonon talk of their text, *The Books of Bokonon,* which shares in the diabolical irreverence of Blake's "The Bible of Hell." Dazed, Bokonon proffers Jonah the final sentence of *The Books of Bokonon,* which is an urging that Jonah write "a history of human stupidity." This is to be written in untruth because in a world of radical instability and deception, inverted language is all that is left for communication. Accordingly, the epigraph to the complete novel runs: "Nothing in this book is true." We are left in *Cat's Cradle* not only with the negation of vision but also with the negation of communication. Solipsism, the final divorce of relations, among persons, is the ruling condition in the novel.

The satirist's job is to poke fun at things, and Vonnegut's ceremonial Author cannot be faulted in this work. Jonah has everyone making fools of themselves and mocks his own attempt to clarify things. This was aptly indicated in the hardcover edition (but not in the Dell paperback) by the mathematical sign for logical conclusion ($\therefore$) that he put at the beginning of each chapter to claim a deductive connection that he does not make. Reason necessarily resists the idea of a planet freezing over with *ice-nine*. In his bafflement Jonah develops a scorn for those who take the world's end solemnly. He teaches the reader how to take a joke, which is not only a way of describing how to read the book but also a way of telling us how to live wisely in the universe. But the great satirist does more than rip things apart; he is, Frye says, "an apocalyptic visionary . . . for his caricature leads us irresistibly away from the passive assumption that the unorganized data of sense experience are reliable and consistent"[9] and invites us to see (and now I cite Blake's *Marriage*) "the infinite which was hid." A change in our perception affords a new kind of contact with the world.

Vonnegut goes about his task in *Cat's Cradle* in the same way. He does not stay with Swift's unattainable idealism. Nor does he posit Blake's glorious mythology of man's resurrection (though he does show the beyond in other books). His view is personalist and immanent. "'Think of what paradise this world would be if men were kind and wise.'" Unfortunately what the novel dramatizes does not share this cheerfulness but rather encourages a judgment that a scientific and utopian belief in the limitless power and perfectibility of human nature is one of those evil illusions by which humankind tries to make life easy and wonderful while actually causing great pain. The proclamation of Vonnegut's Jonah points toward but does not reveal deliverance. He directs us to laugh at the disasters brought about by our scientific and political egotism in order that we may turn away from a prideful death-wish to appreciate what is good in the world and dear in other persons. As Jonah of the Old Testament became a sign to the people of Nineveh, so stands his self-appointed namesake before this generation. In reviving this ancient mode of addressing the human situation, Vonnegut expands his conception of his fiction into an instrument of prophetic reform, a purpose that subtly shapes his forthcoming experimentation.

5

GOD BLESS YOU, MR. ROSEWATER

> The Lord will give strength to his people;
> The Lord will bless his people with peace.
>
> Psalm 29

> Call down blessings on your persecutors—
> blessings, not curses.
>
> Romans 12:14

God Bless You, Mr. Rosewater (1965) is a companion book to *Cat's Cradle*, which was published two years earlier. Both novels show men of good will struggling to make sense of a bewildering, fallen universe by answering the naked needs of others. The locale shifts from the vitiated Caribbean utopia of San Lorenzo in *Cat's Cradle* to humdrum middle America where it is charmingly named Rosewater County, Indiana; but the moral atmosphere remains a place of misery and failure. Vonnegut's fifth novel, *God Bless You, Mr. Rosewater,* brings disaster back home from its imaginary outposts to remind us that collapse is at hand. What is typical about this typical American town is noticed in its array of "shit-houses" and shacks which structuralize the shabby way people live in "this Utopia gone bust." Having discarded in *Cat's Cradle* the efforts of organized religion and science to improve life, and having questioned in *Mother Night* the capacity of art to penetrate the abiding deterioration, Vonnegut moves on to consider the power of money to humanize life through the kind offices of Eliot Rosewater, who oversees the vast resources of the Rosewater Foundation.

Eliot Rosewater's character is a résumé of the qualities Vonnegut developed in the principal figures of the preceding four novels. Eliot is born to privilege and, with Paul Proteus in *Player Piano,* turns against the system, which respects him for extrinsic reasons, in order that he can present himself as a person. Malachi Constant travels all around the solar system in *The Sirens of Titan* for the simple perspective of which his great material wealth deprived him, and the humility Malachi learns becomes the way of life that his fellow millionaire Eliot takes up in his backwater hometown. But noble intentions can boomerang. Howard J. Campbell goes crazy in *Mother Night* by trying to remain patriotic while serving the Nazi enemy. Or the high cause can overwhelm the endeavor to do what is right. Eliot openly works for the good of others, yet his mind gives way under the massive need he serves. He suffers a spiritual version of the global collapse that overtakes Jonah in *Cat's Cradle.* So Eliot knows all the things that the other figures know, but he cares more. *God Bless You, Mr. Rosewater* tells of the moral activism that lies beyond Jonah's paralyzing, dark knowledge of human affliction and loss.

The pervasive poverty in the Vonnegut world is that of love. Warm feeling between persons marks a special moment in his narratives, and there are few such moments. Intimacy is avoided rather than desired, and friendship is a passing bond. Trust of one person by another is so exceptional that we are likely to accept Jonah's isolation as the given condition. Mere awareness of emotional contact indicates a sympathetic figure who invariably comes across as vulnerable and not infrequently as a bit crazed. Where ignorance of emotion is the norm, sensitivity will inevitably seem to be a mental disorder. The masses of automatons crowding Vonnegut's fictions indicate that lovelessness has reached a crisis stage where indiscriminate affection is called for as a cure. Our task now, Malachi Constant says, "'is to love whoever is around to be loved.'" The last word of *The Sirens of Titan* is the first word of *God Bless You, Mr. Rosewater,* which portrays Eliot making a life out of loving whoever is around to be loved. Love on any terms is risky; for Eliot, who tries "'to love people who have no use,'" it is perilous. His acceptance of the hazards accounts for the unusual tone of tenderness that Vonnegut adopts throughout the narration. And with this novel Vonnegut moves on from satire and lament to benediction.

II

God Bless You, Mr. Rosewater is made up of fourteen chapters which trace the history of Eliot's unprecedented social scheme. The events of his experiment progress without the temporal intricacy or the sudden flights to imaginary places that complicate the other novels. There is a cabal to take over the Rosewater Foundation, but neither this consciously trite substory nor the public consequences of Eliot's altruism gives the novel its essential design. Here, as in all Vonnegut's art, the organizing principle derives from the main character's spiritual change. This novel portrays the development of "a Utopian dreamer, a tinhorn saint, an aimless fool," which is Vonnegut's way of saying that it recounts a lover's progress. Eliot's story falls into four movements: preparation (Chapters 1-4); practice (Chapters 5-7); a New England interlude (Chapters 8-11); and fulfillment through dispersion (Chapters 12-14). The first, second, and fourth trace the stages of Eliot's inner growth, while the third, which belongs to the subplot, shows the necessity of his work by universalizing the spiritual poverty he tries to alleviate.

We initially see Eliot as "a flamboyantly sick man" running around America getting himself locked up—in Swarthmore, Pennsylvania, for disorderly conduct, proclaiming to science-fiction writers how much he loves them, jailed in Vashti, Texas, as a suspicious character for mentioning a revolution. Eliot's behavior takes on several meanings. Norman Mushari, a dumpy shyster lawyer, sees it as an opportunity to cash in on the Foundation's charter by getting Eliot officially certified as insane in order to replace him with a related Rosewater he can control. Mushari's greed reduces Eliot to "'this specimen'" that must be adjudged crazy. Mushari's legal co-workers tag Eliot "The Nut," "The Saint," "John the Baptist," and other such conventional putdowns for being what they are not. Senator Lister Ames Rosewater, Eliot's father, believes strongly that the family's good strong blood will see Eliot through his "'experimenting'" by bringing him "'back to his senses any time he's good and ready.'" Neither the lawyer nor the senator takes Eliot seriously, which means regarding him as a particular person with responses of his own. He is dealt with simply because he is rich or because a son must be dealt with in some way. Senator Rosewater's blindness and Mushari's opportunism represent how people exist to one another as extensions of their own private ego, and they further show how the workaday world estranges Eliot by treating his acts of love as pathology.

The narrator works against the public view of Eliot to show the reader that his ailment is neither court evidence nor passing caper but the manifestation of his deep need to find a truly human value to live by. Eliot's frenzy suggests his despair at not being able to find something he can hold on to. It is not that he has lacked possibilities for esteem. His biography, in fact, reads like an American dream story for our time: born the heir to a great American fortune; trained at Loomis and Harvard; distinguished himself in the Infantry during World War II; married a beautiful Parisienne; returned to complete a Harvard law degree and then a doctorate in international law; took over the Foundation; supported the recognized cultural and medical causes—and Eliot is a broken man. What gratifies others fails Eliot. The goals society sets up for success Eliot passes through as inadequacies. After offering the reader a customarily fatuous Senate speech by Lister, whose language could use some mouthwash, on how easy it would be to get the entire nation into moral shape by returning to the rugged way of "sink-or-swim justice," the narrator quietly reminds us of Eliot's helpless state. Eliot, like Campbell when he sentences himself, and like Jonah when he confronts an engulfing ruined world, is friendless. Friendlessness is Vonnegut's darkest state.

Eliot stands in the aloneness that remains when the explanations others have of themselves do not apply to one's own life. He alienates all his friends by systematically telling them that whatever they based their self-respect on is inessential. He dismisses the money of his rich friends as "dumb luck." The work of his artistic friends is sop for the ignorant rich. The ideas of his scholar friends are "'boring crap'"; and he sends his scientist friends away by telling them that their work has improved human life—the bitter fool's sardonic compliment, which even scientists do not expect. Eliot has effectively cut himself off from human sympathy by discarding the grounds upon which our consoling ambitions are built. Two things are left—psychoanalysis, which retools emotional rejects to work smoothly in the social mechanism, and love, the cynic's last resort. Eliot tries both. Therapy brings Eliot to make the surface changes required to get along, such as grooming himself and swearing off alcohol, with the effect of further burying his central need beneath a facade of order. Nor does love work for Eliot, for marriage does not touch that need either. To survive, Eliot's wife Sylvia has begun divorce proceedings, which in

Vonnegut's fiction signals the impingement of the inimical world upon the consecrated nation of two. These are the crises of Eliot's "time of troubles." One evening at the Metropolitan Opera, during the last scene of *Aida,* he explodes. He shouts out to the two stage lovers, sealed in their death-loving tomb, to save oxygen. "'You will last a lot longer, if you don't try to sing.'"

Eliot wants to save people from whatever economical or emotional ailment distresses them. Each of his dissatisfactions prepares him to renounce the power of the world in order to accept a life of service to others. He does not hear voices, but he has the zeal of a missionary. He writes to Sylvia: "There is this feeling that I have a destiny far away from the shallow and preposterous posing that is our life in New York." He sets up shop in Rosewater, Indiana, the ancestral town that was never home for this roamer. Home is to be found; it is karmic geography, not a stamp on a birth certificate. Home is where one's destiny lies.

Eliot's destiny involves a reparation so comprehensive that this tinhorn saint seems to be a genuinely holy person. Settling in the Township of Rosewater puts the historical burden of his family on his shoulders. The town is the shell left by the economic exploitation of his great-grandfather, Noah, and the political exploitation of his father, who refers to his constituency as "'the sniveling camaraderie of whores, malingerers, pimps, and thieves'" and nevertheless uses them as a power base for his ambition. Rosewater is Hometown, U. S. A., for the homeless. He says to his bewildered wife:

"I look at these people, these Americans," Eliot went on, "and I realize that they can't even care about themselves any more—because they have no *use*. The factory, the farms, the mines across the river—they're almost completely automatic now. And America doesn't even need these people for war. . . ."

Rosewater, Indiana, is the American past as American destiny. Here Eliot is brought back to himself as well as to his heritage. Tucked in the recess of his patriarchal complicity lies Eliot's personal responsibility to save others.

During the war in Bavaria he led an attack on a smoke-filled building that was supposedly infested with S. S. troops. He learned soon after rushing in that he had killed three unarmed firemen—two old men with his grenade, and a boy with his bayonet. They had been trying to put out the fire in what was a clarinet factory. Understandably, Eliot does not easily

assuage his guilt for this carnage. Ten minutes after the murders, he lay
down in front of a moving truck, which stopped just in time. Many years
later, in Rosewater, he lays his life down before the troubles of others.
The guilt lingers. To try to make amends, he becomes the spiritual volunteer fireman in Rosewater, ready to answer every human emergency that
comes through his black phone (which is near the red phone he answers
as Fire Lieutenant). Eliot takes on the crimes of his personal and familial
past along with the disasters that are the world's estate. On one side of
Main Street is his firehouse; facing it across the way in a shotgun attic
is the Foundation office with this sign in its two windows:

ROSEWATER FOUNDATION
HOW CAN WE HELP
YOU?

The active phase (Chapters 5-7) of Eliot's dedication to helping others
is counterpointed against a meeting in Washington of the senator, Sylvia,
and lawyers who are discussing a reunion of the couple, now separated for
three years, which may reconcile them and, if the senator can have his
way, produce a male heir to the Rosewater fortune. The negotiations
reveal a warmly sympathetic Sylvia who intellectually supports her husband's humanitarianism but emotionally is unable to handle the misery
to which his work constantly exposes her. The senator and the lawyers
display their expected callousness. Their efforts to profit from the pain
between Sylvia and Eliot prompt the reader to admire Eliot's living out of
his generous convictions. In Indiana he lives as unaccommodated man
without external props of dignity. He subsists alone in the upstairs office
with a single blue chalkstripe suit traded from a volunteer fireman in New
Egypt, New Jersey, surrounded by tax forms for the Foundation, pictures
to cheer people up, assorted minor remedies for major ailments, and "his
uncritical love," which is the fecund minimum of his renunciatory life.
A good deal of Eliot's mission is conducted by telephone. Diana Moon
Glampers calls in the middle of a night thunderstorm to cry that the
electricity is after her again. Then an anonymous man finds the Foundation number in the phone booth and dials it to proclaim, "'I'm worse than
nothing.'" Their terrors are common and easily detonated. Lightning
strikes Diana's sense of worthlessness. She feels that no one would miss
her if she died, and the man challenges Eliot to stop him from killing
himself to see if this extreme act will bring concern. In such crises the

telephone acquires special meaning. It provides the last hope for the isolated self. The phone protects the caller with impersonality while letting that person's voice be heard. Voice is spiritual contact. In Rosewater, Indiana, the meeting of inner human natures can only be approached shyly, for it exposes the tender needs that have been denied. Voice articulates this inwardness in a way that our other gestures do not. Eliot instinctively knows the remarkable power of voice. He speaks in different modes on his two phones, reserving his "sweet, vastly paternal" voice, which is "as humane as the lowest note of a cello," for the black emergency phone. Diana says that her kidneys stop hurting "'just hearing your sweet voice.'" Voice can heal. Eliot's coming into his own humane voice measures the value of his philanthropic experiment. Sylvia rightly calls Eliot a poet.

The lightning and thunder that transform "everything to blue-white diamonds" while Diana and Eliot speak dramatize the larger dimension of Eliot's mission. Lightning signifies God's active presence; thunder is his voice. His mighty crash can terrify Diana and it can strengthen Eliot. Psalm 29, from which this chapter's epigraph is taken, clarifies Vonnegut's technique here. The Psalm traces the thunderstorm across the land through its divisive and creative effects and concludes the analogy between the thunder and God's voice with the life-giving assurance of God's power. "The Lord will give strength to his people; / The Lord will bless his people with peace." In a letter to his wife, Eliot contrasts his having to operate without instructions to Hamlet's being told exactly what to do by his father's ghost; "But from somewhere something is trying to tell me where to go, what to do there. . . ." The theophanies of lightning and thunder are his instructions. Eliot is an instrument of the Father's grace gift of healing and peace. The imagery explicitly underscores this association. When Diana's physical pain and panic stop, the thunder and lightning also cease. "There was only the hopelessly sentimental music of rainfall now." Her profuse gratitude gives the novel its title—"'God Bless You, Mr. Rosewater.'" The duet between Eliot's cello voice and clapping thunder expresses the blessing that Eliot brings to the human devastations of Rosewater, Indiana.

Diana's view of her death is symptomatic of the suicidal disease afflicting many figures in the novel. Eliot himself muses on Hamlet's famous weighing of what it is "not to be" against the paltry benefits of existence. The pathology is serious enough for Kilgore Trout, Eliot's oracular hero, to imagine government-sponsored suicide parlors "at every major intersection, right next door to an orange-roofed Howard Johnson's," replete with Muzak and a death stewardess. Where the death wish is institution-alized, human uselessness is a foregone conclusion. The town of Rose-water is an early stage of this distempered state. Eliot's gentle, curative power is not equal to the malady, although God's thunder would be an equal match. Still, Eliot goes on in the exhausted voice of patient sorrow trying to keep people from killing themselves. If those he helps to stay alive are not as noble as he makes them out to be, they are not as base as his father insists—they are, plainly, human. This simple perception of human nature has so fallen into concealment that its recognition has the force of mystery. When the senator snidely asks Sylvia what keeps Eliot among those people, Sylvia says, "'The secret is that they're human.'"

The account of Eliot's apostolate draws to an end with the intrusion of personal matters. The Mushari plot is thickening, and the senator is pressing for a reconciliation between his son and Sylvia on the vague possibility of their producing a male heir. Though Eliot agrees to meet with her in Indianapolis, he feels that it is "a tremendously dangerous thing for two such sick and loving people to do." He senses the futility of working out a life with the woman he loves. He and Sylvia can only recognize each other in the stale grandeur of failed love, each deepening the vulnerability of the other. This second sequence closes as Eliot's spirit lifts in anticipation of baptizing a baby the next day. "'There's only one rule that I know of, babies,'" he will say while sprinkling water. "'God damn it, you've got to be kind.'" His words ceremonialize the needs of others flowing into his own. Paradoxically, it is McAllister of the law firm McAllister, Robjent, Reed and McGee, which makes a business of prevent-ing saintliness among its clients, who gives the context of Eliot's goodness when McAllister disdainfully compares a rich man's initial desire to allevi-ate suffering with having his nose rubbed in the Sermon on the Mount for the first time. Jesus' crucial sermon, it exhorts his followers to show charity through a secret almsgiving.

The third sequence (Chapters 8-11) is in manner a throwback to the social jabbing Vonnegut does handily. The action shifts to Pisquontuit, Rhode Island—pronounced "Piss-on-it" by its detractors—home of Eliot's second cousin, Fred Rosewater, whom Mushari hopes to put in Eliot's place as head of the Foundation. But Mushari's cabal can no more effect-ively enter the main action than Mushari can rise above his legalistic sycophancy. Mushari remains a minor character in a tale whose protagonist is money. When money is "a leading character," to stay with the novel's open-ing statement about itself, we have the American Dream. The Pisquontuit episode adds a chapter to our ongoing tribal epic. This town has arrived at that advanced affluent state at which point money fulfills for its citizens the function that history and myth and work and wisdom served in less evolved societies.

Beneath Pisquontuit's surface difference from Rosewater, Indiana, there lies a radical kinship. The wealthy who do not have to work are mirror images of the poor Rosewaterites who are not able to work. The Pine Tree Press of the Freedom School publishes a pamphlet attacking the beneficiaries of social security and welfare. The reactionary argument perfectly describes the recipients of endowed welfare systems flourishing under the tax dodge called trust fund. The tract is its own critique:

They do not work and will not. Heads down, unmindful, they have neither pride nor self-respect. They are totally unreliable, not maliciously so, but like cattle who wander aimlessly. Foresight and the ability to reason have simply atrophied from long neglect. Talk to them, listen to them, work with them as I do and you realize with a kind of dull horror that they have lost all semblance of human beings except that they stand on two feet and talk—like parrots. "More. Give me more. I need more," are the only new thoughts they have learned. . . .

Two qualities mark life that is no longer recognizably human—artificiality and enslavement. In Pisquontuit, fakery appeals to people more than authenticity. Bunny Weeks's restaurant *The Weir* and adjoining gift shop *The Jolly Whaler* sentimentally replicate the very nautical setting they are in as though the setting were inadequate. Harpoons lie across rafters; patrons may order the Horse Mackerel Cocktail and Fisherman's Salad to bring them into the fishing business vicariously. Decor extracts life from the real thing by making it artificial. Invariably, human emotion rises to the stylized occasion, at which level feeling becomes falsified. The authentic then comes off as unreal. Bunny treats Harry Pena and his sons, who are genuine fishermen, as idle entertainment for his dinner patrons. "'That's all over, men working with their hands and backs. They are not needed,'" quips the restaurateur. When describing the fisherman as having gone "fishing for real fish with his two real sons—in a real boat on a salty sea," the narrator through style tries to rescue reality from Bunny's imprisoning fabrications.

Life led at a remove from actuality is desperate, and despair is a function of money in Pisquontuit. Stewart Buntline, heir to the Buntline broom and tobacco fortune, is told by his attorney that without his wealth he would not be getting the priceless time of a senior partner. Time of others is all his money brings. We see Buntline near forty, enervated in his study, too stupefied to touch the flat Scotch and soda next to him. Selena, the Buntlines' upstairs maid, lives in virtual chattel servitude, since she was raised in an orphanage the Buntlines founded in 1878 as a training center for their domestic staff. And Fred Rosewater, the poor insurance salesman from the wrong side of the Rosewater line, looks constantly for an external ratification of his worth. He momentarily rejoices to learn in a family history book that he has noble Scot blood until he finds that termites ate the heart out of the book. Then he calmly decides to hang himself. "He was worth forty-two thousand dollars dead."

Collectively, the New England and midwestern towns suggest that life in America now goes on in two ways: there are the poor who serve the rich, and there are the rich who serve their money. Where money is king, all people are slaves. Diana's trap is economic and emotional. Selena can be a rich servant so long as she remains a poor person. The slave bracelet Bunny Weeks wears merely embellishes his captivity. Pisquontuit universalizes the suffering seen earlier in Rosewater County so that the problem of loving people who have no use seems to be a national emergency. Eliot takes on this need as a moral responsibility, and elects poverty, choosing to be a poor servant of others in order to be rich as a person.

The closing movement of the novel (Chapters 12-14) is a pageant of farewells: goodbye to Rosewater County as Eliot packs his bag to meet Sylvia in Indianapolis; a final leave-taking, really, because the Mushari lawsuit requires that Eliot end this part of his life to prove his sanity; and then a departure from sanity as his burdened mind sinks into the serenity of breakdown; in a mental hospital a year later with a parting shot he settles the legal confusion by writing a check to his rival and declaring himself father to all fifty-seven claimants to his paternity; and by the wondrous sway of love these farewells are transformed into the closing hello of harmony.

Two images dramatize the importance of these valedictions for Eliot's spiritual growth. The first depicts Eliot as a clown. Attired in uncomfortably new clothing that crackles as though lined with newspaper, he tramps toward the bus terminal with the jaunty steps of "a Chaplinesque *boulevardier*," patting the heads of the dogs welcoming him on the street. In the novel's final scene at the hospital someone dressed him "for tennis, all in snowy white . . . as though he were a department store display." His costumes are meant to impress the world with his sanity, but they are the uniform of pathetic conventionality draped on the shell of a person. Ludicrous incongruity, not sanity, emanates from his appearance. The mannequin perfection calls attention to Eliot's shattered state of being involved with his deepest self, involved with what is most solitary and therefore altogether unreachable. If all people are fools in the eyes of God, then we have just such a privileged view here. Eliot stands as the human person in innocence, a Chaplin hugging the truths of the heart. One such truth is that love makes Eliot dangerously vulnerable. His father accuses him of hatred; the human world moves in grasping and injurious ways and so regards him as mad. Eliot Rosewater, the rueful fool, painted and broken, stands as a critique of our rational, heartless, mechanized society.

Disaster, the second image, pictures the loveless world. The town of Rosewater, already in economic shambles, panics at the thought of Eliot's pulling out forever. The image of ruin expands as Eliot rides away. He reads of the death of the entire Milky Way in Kilgore Trout's *Pan-Galactic Three-Day Pass.* His calm while reading is broken, on the outskirts of Indianapolis, by the apocalyptic image bursting alive with the entire city "being consumed by a fire-storm." The infernal vision takes his now scorched imagination back to a vividly recalled description of Dresden going up in a column of fire. These imagined disasters comprise a clown-scape showing the insuperable odds Eliot is up against, and the havoc foreshadows the barrenness left by the evacuation of his ardor. The image also externalizes his inner heat. Once warm with affection for others, it is eventually cooled by Eliot's dampening sense of having hurt Sylvia and his father in the name of love. The comic figure limned against wreckage defines the triumph born of loss. Eliot ends up a fool of love. He renews the world by becoming one of the disgraced and the ridiculous whom he tried to help. Vonnegut's comic spirit at the end tells us how to read Eliot's magical closing gesture of giving away money and making heirs of the children of Rosewater who claim to be his offspring. It is not to be taken as a contrivance or a contradiction but as a transcendence, which is the formal way fairy tales and miracle stories end. Generosity lifts the reader out of the topsy-turvy world of enslaving power into the world of instinctive love.

The narrative voice sympathetically registers Eliot's change from lover to saint and finally to fool and madman. The tone remains approving while Eliot turns against his class and deepens in compassion during his activism. During the Pisquontuit interlude, the tone becomes gently mocking until Eliot breaks down and tries to pull himself together, at which time the voice is openly celebratory. The narrator yields to Kilgore Trout, society's "'greatest prophet,'" to validate the importance of Eliot's life. It does not go without saying that such work is valuable or even respectable, so Trout says it, doing unto Eliot what he has done unto others:

Well . . . what you did in Rosewater County was far from insane. It was quite possibly the most important social experiment of our time, for it dealt on a very small scale with a problem whose queasy horrors will eventually be made world-wide by the sophistication of machines. The problem is this: How to love people who have no use?

What Eliot does is to give life. A woman caller, whose anonymity suggests that she speaks for all his clients, says about his departure: "'Oh, Mr. Rosewater—if you go away and never come back, we'll die.'" Her pitiful dependence on Eliot's presence acknowledges his life-giving power.

By going back to the novel's title after tracing Eliot's change, we can bring together the differences between his sense of life and that of others. The title *God Bless You, Mr. Rosewater* comes from a common expression, usually our automatic response to sneezing; but the phrase essentially derives from a solemn utterance, the blessing. The blessing is originally conceived of as a communication of life from God. With life come well-being and success, which are the bases for peace of mind and peace in the world. Though only God can bless, people can bless by asking that God will bless. Eliot's ministry of love distributes blessings extravagantly. When he explains his work with the poor to his father, "the Senator cursed." When Eliot tenderly asks about his cursing, "the Senator cursed again" to which Eliot responds: "'I love you so.'" Cursing and swearing recur throughout the novel. They are the rhetoric of the blasphemed life. And life for many on Earth is a condemnation. For Delbert Peach, the town drunk, "his efforts to stop being a human being and become a dog" are a desire to move up the evolutionary scale. As Eliot returns a blessing for his father's many curses, he neutralizes the anti-life around him with hope. If we come to think of Eliot as living out Jesus' commandment to his disciples to answer the curse with a blessing, as Vonnegut seems to invite us to do, then we can sense the seriousness in the bitter comic ending. In the Bible the Father communicates life to his Son. Passing on life is the essential blessing. In the end Eliot does just this to his fifty-seven new, stray children: "'And tell them . . . to be fruitful and multiply.'"

These are the last words of the novel. They suspend the action in a mandate for regeneration. If only for this closing moment, love harmonizes the social disorder with which the story began. Eliot's presence assures us that there is one entirely good man in the world. The gesture magically shows that cruelty and confusion are merely at the service of order and goodness. The miracle Eliot performs does not wipe away the world's havoc. Chaos abides; it is the law of nature. His miracle amounts to correcting our vision; for his life teaches us that we have only to alter the way we look at the world to accept its unpredictability and to recognize the humanness in people through their need for affectionate contact. Eliot's potentiality has been intimated all along in the name Rosewater, which hints of gentleness, fairness, and transformation. The final wonder that Vonnegut observes is the transformation in Eliot's spirit. At the end he is not the lunatic philanthropist casting pearls before swine, to borrow from the novel's sardonic subtitle; nor is he the helpless madman cast in the prison of his mind or behind the bars of psychic conventionality. Rather, he is the good man casting life onto the world. The typographical display of Eliot's initial *R* scattered throughout the printed text with asterisks (stars, really) recalls his baptismal sprinkling of life-giving water on Mary Moody's twins, and comes to mark how the fruits of his moral imagination fall as a benediction on the entire novelistic world. Besides its creative implication, blessing may refer to the power inherent in the spoken words, to the words themselves, and to their effects. Eliot's words augur health, progeny, prosperity, harmony, victory over adversity, and wisdom. These are rare gifts. In wishing them for others, Eliot receives the greatest gift of all: he becomes the lover he had the courage to imagine himself to be.

6

SLAUGHTERHOUSE-FIVE

> Each person completely touches us
> With what he is and as he is,
> In the stale grandeur of annihilation.
>
> Wallace Stevens, *Lebensweisheitspielerei*

In 1969 when *Slaughterhouse-Five* was published, Vonnegut came into his own as a novelist. We are still in the wake of enthusiasm that greeted the book, for readers and critics then began the serious reevaluation of his earlier books which has succeeded in establishing Vonnegut as a major American writer. And the more we learn about his larger achievement, the more prominent *Slaughterhouse-Five* becomes. It is the story of the gratuitous Allied air attack on Dresden, Germany, on February 13, 1945, in which a cultural center and nonmilitary city were fire-bombed into utter ruin. Vonnegut went through the conflagration as a prisoner of war and was never able to shake the experience loose from his memory. As the novel brought him fame, it also brought him to himself by expressing the suppressed pain of the massacre, which had been lurking unvoiced in his imagination all the while he was writing books about fictitious disasters.

What I believe is most important for an understanding of *Slaughterhouse-Five* and for a study of Vonnegut's artistry is how his change of heart in directly confronting his subject brings about a change in the form of his fiction. In fact, the question of novelistic form is equated in the book with the task of writing about Dresden. The reader is forced to consider the very nature of the book that he is involved in through reading, just as

Vonnegut forces himself to look squarely at his hellish knowledge. One scene illustrates my point. Billy Pilgrim, the time-traveler, has learned a lesson on the planet Tralfamadore that he believes can give peace to the troubled lives of his fellow earthlings. He wanders into a radio talk show that is considering whether or not the novel is dead. The spectacle comes off as intrusive both in its narrative placing and in the critical language of the panel, whose members' stupidity deepens the suspicion that the novel is an idle undertaking. The scene is so contrived that we are likely to dismiss it unless we allow that Vonnegut is addressing himself to that hyperconsciousness toward his own work. Survival is what *Slaughterhouse-Five* is all about, and so to take up the question of the novel's survival links form to action: the problem of living through the fire-bombing of Dresden is rivaled by the problem of writing about it. The two acts are analogues, and from the tone of the passage on the viability of fiction we can pick up Vonnegut's meaning. He is not quite predicting a future for the novel but he is negating its death notice. He is not quite prescribing a function for the novel, but he is deriding the cheap purposes it has been made to serve. We are at least made aware that the life of form relates to the form of our lives. Vonnegut comments on the reality of Dresden by treating the problems of fiction.

This indirect formulation of the novel's function expresses Vonnegut's approach to art. He questions the mold he uses. He begins *before* the first sentence of the story. The title page undermines our expectation about design with three titles. The proper one refers to a pig slaughterhouse in Dresden, which housed American prisoners in World War II. The second shows how language falsifies war: "The Children's Crusade" transforms brutality into sentimental heroism, calculation into innocence. The third title, "A Duty-Dance with Death," borrows from Céline to state that art must confront death frankly. The use of three titles effectively denies the adequacy of any one title for the book. Instead of a label we are given a deepening attitude toward the violence of war. The formal and typographical confusions underscore this dislocation. The title page reads like a prayer and looks like a poster. Outlined, the words become a bomb. The final word, "PEACE," caps the plea of an exhausted survivor.

The novel proper tells the story of survival. There are ten chapter-like sections, covering Vonnegut's life from just before the Dresden attack in 1945, through the bombing, and into postwar life in America. This is the bare chronology of the story. Despite the numerous skips and turns of Vonnegut's memory, the reader can discern this time pattern, but only faintly, for clock time is not the basis for the unity of a tale announced as "telegraphic schizophrenic." The mnemonic order is complicated by two strategies. First, autobiography gives way to biography. The opening and closing chapters are the only sequences dealing with Vonnegut himself. Early in the book he abandons his story to tell about a fellow American, Billy Pilgrim, whom he met in a Dresden prison camp. The memoir Vonnegut planned is discarded as impossible to write for his imagination boggles before the holocaust of 135,000 human lives. His scrapping of the plan (the failure of that form) is not antecedent to the story but essential to the novel's action.

The second strategy emerges from the curious materials making up the novel. The book comes to the reader as a collage with mere silhouettes of human figures. "There are almost no characters in this story, and almost no dramatic confrontations, because most of the people in it are so sick and so much the listless playthings of enormous forces. One of the main effects of war, after all, is that people are discouraged from being characters." And so graffiti, war memos, anecdotes, jokes, songs—light operatic and liturgical—raw statistics, assorted tableaux, flash before the reader's eye like frames on a fragmented cinematic documentary. Even the clipped paragraphical shapes show the limited units of the novel's progression. The shards of prose seem uniformly important, or unimportant, claiming no more significance than does the bird talk ending the first and last chapters: "One bird said to Billy Pilgrim, 'Poo-tee-weet?'" Massacres defy explanation. Old forms are shattered. The world is cuckoo. Accordingly, the reader is left with an image of twittering unintelligibility summing up what the dispersed narrative momentum anticipated in many ways—refusing to reach a crisis or resolution, refusing, in fine, to clarify itself or its intention for the reader.

The strategies that entangle *Slaughterhouse-Five* also offer clues to how its disparateness comes together. The shift, from the narrator's own predicament to Billy Pilgrim's, alters the perspective from introspection to observation, thereby making Vonnegut the narrator into a confessing witness. The implications here are several. Detached at the same time that he is sympathetic to Billy's experience, the narrator can suggest a way of seeing, through compassionate wisdom, the otherwise baffling war in the context of other catastrophes. The hurt and wonder of Billy's life become the hurt and wonder of every time. And there is a moral quality to this change of perspective. The testimony of the witness is anchored in an ability to move out of self-absorption into the suffering of another. A series of Old and New Testament allusions identifies the moral impact of this gesture.

The biblical motif is a perfect instance of a shaping allusion which readers must approach as they would a poetic device. The force of the motif derives from a slow gathering of its elements. The most important biblical reference in the novel is to the Gospels. It first arises through stylistic parody. Recalling a trip to New York City with his daughter and her friend, Vonnegut perceives the technological trap Americans define themselves by. "We went to the New York World's Fair, saw what the past had been like according to the Ford Motor Car Company and Walt Disney, saw what the future would be like, according to General Motors." The incantatory repetition of *according to* exposes the tacit demand that capitalistic technology be affixed to the other four versions of the Gospels. Science in our time has become a source of moral imperatives addressed to our deepest spiritual needs. The witness shows how technology contributes to and responds to our sense of crisis. It even provides a revision of the Jesus stories. Kilgore Trout, a specialist in exposing the undercurrents of our thinking, writes *The Gospel from Outer Space* to correct what he regards as "slipshod storytelling" in the New Testament, thereby teaching people "to be merciful, even to the lowest of the low." As we can tell from the model of the Gospels that Trout revises, the rival of science for belief is Christianity. Now Christianity has shaped the lives of these characters as deeply as has science; so the central events from the Gospels provide a backdrop for the story of Billy Pilgrim. The birth, ministry, and passion of Jesus remind us of the disenfranchised and disturbing person behind the historical institution bearing his name: "Jesus really *was* a nobody, and a pain in the neck to a lot of people with better connections than he had."

If we pause briefly to consider the original nature of the Christian Gospels, what may strike the reader as another of Vonnegut's ironic invocations will open a way into the novel. Simply, the word *gospel* translates from the Greek for good tidings *(euangelion)*. The specific good tidings are of victory over death through the resurrection of Jesus. The Gospels prepare humanity to face its end. Though *gospel* refers to purpose, it also describes a form. The Gospels are an amalgamation of language forms that were available to the early Christians to spread their good tidings, rather than a fixed, ideal shape sent down out of the blue. Sermon, prophecy, the Old Testament, psalm, prayer, legend, parable, apothegm, miracle story, and the sayings of Jesus were all used. To win followers the evangelists drew on whatever verbal means were at hand in their popular culture. Karl Kundsin, a pioneer in New Testament research, writes that the saving message "is, as a whole, to be judged as a kind of childlike stammering about the Absolute, as a speaking in tongues, which may indeed often seem to us mere confusion, on account of its multiplicity of meaning...."[1] The old forms were inadequate to convey the momentous news, so primitive Christians made their own. From tradition, by breaking inherited molds, through the manifold and imperfect forms of their community the evangelists delivered the word of God as it was embodied in the unsettling life of Jesus.

An equally sharp awareness of calamity pervades *Slaughterhouse-Five,* leading to a comparably innovative feeling for form. The story, like the story of Jesus, is apocalyptic in that its prophetic revelation is given under the duress of the end, a massive end—the end of human life, and end of the world, the end, also, of form. The structural variety that comes to the reader is a manifestation of Vonnegut's sense of end-time, for he has drawn bits and pieces of leftover forms in our popular culture to shape his testimony. We can see now the existential range implied by his modest meditation on the World's Fair: "And I asked myself about the present: how wide it was, how deep it was, how much was mine to keep." *Slaughterhouse-Five,* like the Gospels, is an exploration of our moment in relation to death through the broken forms defining the dimensions of our presentness.

I I

In the rest of this chapter I will consider the novel as moral testimony, using three lines of discussion: first, the way Vonnegut the witness draws moral force by undermining conventional narrative authority; second, the nature and life of Billy Pilgrim, who exemplifies the teachings of the testimony; and, finally, the rivaling gospels or truths determining how we live. From there I will suggest the dynamics of the novel's form.

Slaughterhouse-Five opens with numerous snagged beginnings that produce a humility rite for Vonnegut through a confession of inadequacy. The fire-bombing of Dresden, which was an open city without defense or military importance, proves inexplicable to him. A recent visit to the city deepens his anxiety, for he finds that modern technology has remade a Baroque art center into a Dayton, Ohio. He tries to outline the Dresden story but comes up with child's play. Calamity becomes decoration; orange cross-hatchings on a roll of wallpaper insult the 135,000 lives consumed in the holocaust. Tourist guides and histories are nostalgic forms to a city that is no more. Vonnegut then turns inward to ponder the moral geography limned by the devastated physical one. Roethke and Céline are promptings toward honesty, but only that. As a last resort he goes to Genesis, the story of first things, to learn from other holocausts in other times. But the raining of fire and brimstone on Sodom and Gomorrah in the Old Testament seems a just act compared to the airplane assaults on Dresden simply for being there, vulnerable and beautiful.

No wonder the first words of the novel proclaim fallibility. "All this happened, more or less." The opening words introduce an unstable verisimilitude where merge true and false, past and future, here and there, inner space and outer space. This coalescing on many levels carries with it a repudiation of facts that makes our reading an ironic exercise. We learn to distrust history. Historical judgment is founded in causality, which this novel negates. The last word of history is the first word of *Slaughterhouse-Five*. We see the wiping out of "The Florence on the Elbe" as so gratuitous, so nihilistic that to call it victory, as history does, debases language. The facts of the bombing are pointedly confused in the novel. Actually a British plan, in the novel it seems an American scheme. The effect of blurring facts shifts the emphasis from political settlement to moral outcome. In moral terms, we are all responsible for the slaughter. And as we follow the narrator-witness through postwar American life, we lose any sense that the country won World War II.

Vonnegut's testimony puts a moral light on war to reveal alliances not shown by treaties. The essential battle here is waged by man against the violent bent in himself. Vonnegut plumbs the dark forces in the human spirit. Sentimentality, egotism, blind patriotism, materialism, these are the enemy; and for Vonnegut they are the signal qualities of American life. Against them stand conscience and feeling. Vonnegut, the witness, acts as a moral scout, smuggling himself across battle lines to reach the front of consciousness where he hopes to find final resistance to killing. His moral awareness accounts for the uncommon affection for a cherished city of the declared enemy and for the German people themselves. They are presented as fellow human beings struggling against their own propensity for violence. And to the degree that Americans yielded to their destructive urge (the violent style of postwar American life suggests a *high* degree), they—we—fell victims. Both political sides lost in the struggle for human decency.

As the Gospels use the Old Testament, so the novel uses an Old Testament figure to characterize the moral stance of the witness to Dresden. "I've finished my war book now," Vonnegut says at the end of the first chapter. "The next one I write is going to be fun. This one is a failure, and had to be, since it was written by a pillar of salt." The model of survival is Lot's wife who, the novel explains, was turned into a pillar of salt for looking back on the smoldering ruins of Sodom and Gomorrah, which she had escaped. Though spared by God's mercy, she suffered from the warmth of her own mercy. Vonnegut, the witness to Dresden, whose survival from disaster is also his fate, draws strength from seeing how a gesture of helpless love redefines its fatal expression. Once again, the reader sees that failure can be positive in effect on others. Where triumph is born of slaughter, defeat can hold dignity by preserving our capacity to care for others. The Old Testament allusion locates the novel's tonal center at the edge of devastation in a state of grief. The evocation of Lot's wife is technically apt, too. She endured a great deal but knew little, so the pillar of salt protects the novel from settling into the inaccuracies of rationality or conclusiveness.

The narrator-witness evangelizes for love by telling the life not of a savior of the world but of a hapless wanderer through the universe. Billy Pilgrim is a man of our time who floats through events, taking the shape they give him. He is a middle-American. He was born in 1922, the year of Vonnegut's birth, son of a barber in the direful city of Ilium, New York, serves in World War II, then prospers as an optometrist in a suburban shopping center, drives an El Dorado Coupe deVille with bumper stickers encouraging people to support our local police and to visit the Ausable Chasm and, between those devotions, to impeach Earl Warren. The scenario for The Good Life has a part for him. Billy owns his piece of the action in which the American bourgeois success drama is now played—"a fifth of the new Holiday Inn out on Route 54, and half of three Tastee-Freeze stands." And Billy is a family man. Married to Valencia Merble, he has fathered one daughter, Barbara, and one son, Robert, a decorated Green Beret who got "all straightened out" in Vietnam from his exuberant pastimes, such as tipping over tombstones. The Pilgrims' home once even had a dog named Spot running around it. The underside of Billy's life follows the other formula of our time: mental breakdown, shock therapy, emptiness.

Billy's life is so stereotypical that an account of it inevitably takes on a contemptuous tone that conceals his specialness. For one thing, he, like

Eliot Rosewater, is gentle despite pressure to be competitive and cruel. During the war he is a friendless servant to servicemen—"a valet to a preacher, expected no promotions or medals, bore no arms, and had a meek faith in a loving Jesus which most soldiers found putrid." Many survived the war; Billy survived with his tender concern for others intact. For him knowledge is for sharing, not controlling others. One night in 1967 he is mysteriously kidnapped by a flying saucer to the planet Tralfamadore. He asks his green hosts on Tralfamadore: "'So tell me the secret so I can take it back to Earth and save us all: How can a planet live at peace?'" The message from outer space and his commitment to preach it are other marks of Billy's distinctiveness.

The Tralfamadorians do not answer the question verbally, but they do respond by closing "their little hands on their eyes." They demonstrate how to live at peace: concentrate on the happy moments of life and ignore the unhappy ones or "stare only at pretty things as eternity failed to go by." The Tralfamadorian technique of managing pain recalls the way a child may exercise some control over the environment through vision. Shutting the eyes creates the blank which serves to wipe out undesired incidents. The habit may liberate the person from pain; but it may also isolate, because the disappearance of unwelcome sights sets the beholder apart from the universe that is banished. Separated from the actuality it transforms, fantasy can be destructively overwhelming to the dreaming mind. We will see in *Slaughterhouse-Five,* as we saw in the engulfing pretense in *Mother Night,* that self-blinding may create a swift regression to a death-like unconsciousness. Great psychic risk, then, accompanies the inner peace that Billy learns how to develop on Tralfamadore.

The benefit of the new tranquility is not only a release from danger but also a privileged glimpse into time. Disparate moments from the past and from the future can be projected onto the blank made by the covering of eyes. Billy takes many trips through the fourth dimension; each of them permits him to see as whole and coherent his otherwise fragmented life. He can go to sleep a widower and wake up on his wedding day; he walks through a door in 1955, goes out another in 1941, and goes back through that same door in 1963. "'The Tralfamadorians can look at all the different moments just the same way we can look at a stretch of the Rocky Mountains. . . .'"

Billy's pleasant experience on Tralfamadore is complemented by Kilgore Trout's *The Gospel from Outer Space,* given to him by Eliot Rosewater, a fellow veteran suffering a similar mental collapse. Trout's book concerns a visitor "shaped very much like a Tralfamadorian" who on coming to Earth sees a flaw in the New Testament's emphasis on the divinity of Jesus at the expense of the rest of humanity and goes on to revise the historical Gospels to suit the present needs of the suffering nobodies of the world by teaching their potential divine adoption. No longer can lynchers nail a nobody to a cross and get away with it:

. . . just before the nobody died, the heavens opened up, and there was thunder and lightning. The voice of God came crashing down. He told the people that he was adopting the bum as his son, giving him the full powers and privileges of The Son of the Creator of the Universe throughout all eternity. God said this: *From this moment on, He will punish horribly anybody who torments a bum who has no connections!*

The new Gospel makes the world safe for the spiritually disenfranchised. Its saving message is the consolation that the fragments made from living on Earth recommend a person to God. Trout's theology from outer space enables Billy Pilgrim to comprehend himself as one who is set apart from other persons to be included in the drama of salvation. The new Gospel makes life possible for him because it does not deny his paltriness.

Slaughterhouse-Five leaves no doubt that the science-fiction world of Tralfamadore helps Billy. But in a work whose skepticism toward science and technology runs deep and whose style makes the largest possible claim for ambivalence, we would do well to consider the teachings of Trout's *The Gospel from Outer Space* more fully than its fantasy truths would invite. The validity of Trout's Gospel derives from the structure of the world producing it. Outer space lies outside of time. We can evaluate the new Gospel and the Tralfamadorian message by observing the effects on Billy of making time a function of seeing. When his experiences are lined up like so many mountains before his eyes, good and bad moments stand without individual emphasis. Mental disposition is a matter of picking and choosing. So happiness, the desired state, arises not from inner fulfillment but from external visual selection, focusing on "pretty things as eternity failed to go by." By ignoring moments that threaten to crash in on him, such as war, Billy gains control over them. The disquieting experience is there but he is spared its devastating effect. This negating way of handling pain alters Billy's deepest experience of his own being. He can abdicate any need to explain the world around him because moments locked in their discreteness present a world without causality. Fear disappears because fear is causality internalized, molded by an expectation of danger. Where effects do not connect with causes, ambition, anxiety, and anger cannot be felt. Without a measurement between effects there is no change. Finally, the mind masters death, the ultimate change. Billy is forever ready for the shot from a high-powered laser gun that kills him. He reports his several encounters with his murder in calm tones on a tape recorder: *"I, Billy Pilgrim . . . will die, have died, and always will die on February thirteenth, 1976."* The veteran of Dresden dies precisely on the thirty-first anniversary of the fire-bombing.

Billy's death moment is further revealing. The backhanded salute to the nation's bicentennial measures the completeness with which Billy's painful middle-class story is a product of American political history, which has been a chronicle of aggressive pursuit of money and violence. The circumstances of his murder epitomize the violence at large in America. Billy is preaching to a large crowd of prospective converts in Chicago on his favorite Tralfamadorian subjects of time and flying saucers, and we can recognize the riotous 1968 Chicago Democratic Convention turned into revival meeting with the side act of assassination that frequently punctuates our history. The reader is not surprised that Earth should make and unmake Billy so barbarously. We see, too, that his new technique of blinking away unpleasant moments fails to moderate the pain of the event. The horror show is made more horrible by Billy's supercool rendering of his annihilation. Tralfamadorian detachment consoles by denying death, but the absence of Billy's terror is itself a terror. Only by removing emotion can he deal with the world.

The self created by science fiction lacks the tension that makes people human. Billy's estrangement from the world and from himself requires new ways of understanding because the events are too bizarre for his old notions of free will and responsibility; but Tralfamadorian wisdom does not go beyond negation. It acknowledges absurdity and it does less immediate damage to his mind than do the convulsions of electroshock therapy he undergoes at the hospital and the subsequent shock-treatment of bourgeois comfort, but it leaves him insentient. The new Gospel, then, is an equivocal document. It is what it comes from: all is space, so it addresses the spatialized, one-dimensional person. The so-called happy moments are based on lack of emotion.

The genial manner of Billy's green friends disguises the violence submerged in their apathy. They, and not earthlings playing with bombs, bring an end to the universe. (Another blow to the human ego.)

"How—how *does* the Universe end?" said Billy.

"We blow it up, experimenting with new fuels for our flying saucers. A Tralfamadorian test pilot presses a starter button, and the whole Universe disappears." So it goes.

Their apocalyptic calm is born of total indifference. Since they do not change, they have no ethical reference. The opposite of Lot's wife, they know a great deal but care not at all. They play God but without his merciful concern for creation. The Tralfamadorian self embodies the scientific ideal and thereby exposes its shortcoming. The fiction about science is that it acts in a moral vacuum; the truth is that when doing so, science creates that vacuum. These truths we know from *Cat's Cradle*. Tralfamadore is a grim world of mechanical wizardry and moral impoverishment, a World's Fair writ large without anyone around sensible enough to question its appalling impassiveness. We can see why Billy is drawn to the new Gospel: it reinvents his person according to the functional specifications of technology. At the same time, we are alerted that Billy's desire to free himself from the destructive forces of actual earthly life ends with a Tralfamadorian unfeeling reduction to it.

Billy's need to remake himself is never questioned; the manner in which he does so is. Both Billy and Eliot Rosewater "were dealing with similar crises in similar ways. They had both found life meaningless, partly because of what they had seen in war. . . . So they were trying to re-invent themselves and their universe." The ascendency of science fiction implies a failure of Christianity, which serves as model for Trout's new Gospel. Men are caught between two testaments. One is from a remote ancient world; the other from a far-out contemporary world. Both testaments are crucial, for they shape Billy's person. The novel invites us to consider their claims and the foundations of selfhood they lay.

The New Testament reckons time from Jesus' birth. Time is a motion backward and forward. The backward flow is preparation for Jesus: the forward thrust from his birth, as our calendars indicate, is toward the End. The self of Christianity is, then, precisely timed. "This is the seriousness of time and timing," Tillich says. "Through our timing God times the coming of His kingdom; through our timing He elevates the time of vanity into the time of fulfillment."[2] As there are two times, there are two selves, the vain one of this world which is transformed into a self of the eschaton beyond time. Vonnegut implies that the Christian Gospel sense of time seems inadequate to transform our lives. On the one hand, the End has not yet happened, though it was pronounced imminent nearly 2000 years ago, so we take the apocalyptic imagination and its redemptive hope less seriously. On the other hand, having witnessed of late The War To End All Wars, The Third Reich, Dresden (135,000 dead), Tokyo (83,793), Hiroshima (71,379), Vietnam (to be calculated), we have adopted a post-apocalyptic callousness about the modern situation. What End can rival what we have already witnessed?[3]

The Gospel from Outer Space does speak to our sense of crisis by proposing an eschatology of the single moment. Our sense of collapse is ratified by its nominalism. Its appeal, however, expresses its limitation. "If what Billy Pilgrim learned from the Tralfamadorians is true," Vonnegut says, "that we will all live forever, not matter how dead we may sometimes seem to be, I am not overjoyed." A self without death is a self without transcendence. Trout's new Gospel gives destruction history where the Christian Gospels offer salvation history.

There is, in sum, a tension among three shaping forces in *Slaughterhouse-Five:* the ancient Christian news of victory over death; the Tralfamadorian message of no death; and the message implied in the reader's unfolding consciousness about the respective choices of each message. This deepening consciousness is Vonnegut's gospel. I would put their respective views of self in this way: whereas the Christian self exists between vanity and fulfillment, the science-fiction self is eternally in isolation. Vonnegut, working against both views, seeks to measure the self's relatedness in mutuality through its capacity to grow in consciousness and compassion. Vonnegut's new covenant stipulates the obligation of spiritual nurturance among persons.

I I I

The form of *Slaughterhouse-Five* is an act of the mind. Visualize the stretch of Rocky Mountains that renders the Tralfamadorian time scheme —moments permanently fixed in separate risings and fallings. Then set the curve in motion. This is the novel's movement, a serpentine line with beginning joined to ending as the tail of the oriental serpent coils toward its mouth. In the spirit of self-commentary and self-plagiarism that runs through Vonnegut's books, the succeeding, companion novel *Breakfast of Champions* (1973) uses the serpent to describe time in a way that accounts for the illuminating experience of reading *Slaughterhouse-Five.*

"What is time?" Vonnegut muses, playing Creator of the Universe in *Breakfast of Champions.* "It is a serpent which eats its tail, like this," and he appends his own illustration of the serpent that resembles a cross-section of a car tire.

Billy's mind provides the technique to propel this movement. As war split his being, so Vonnegut recounts the events in disjointed fragments; and as war discourages people from being themselves, dramatic confrontation is minimized. The challenge of form is made to the reader who is required to unify this narrative manqué. The dramatic energy is rechanneled toward the reader, who becomes another collaborating pilgrim achieving a progress of awareness denied Billy Pilgrim.

One conspicuous gesture used to mark the events is the phrase *so it goes* after any reference to death. The phrase actually seems to work against continuity because it breaks the action right at the point that seems to require extension if we are to understand death with more than Tralfamadorian disregard. By recalling the scriptural derivation, however, we can respond to the unity of effect created by the phrase. *So it goes* is a close translation of *amen,* which is Hebrew for "truly" or "it is true." Through Jesus' use of it in the Gospels, *amen* signifies a solemn affirmation of God's presence binding the course of events: *so be it, let it be that way.* The phrase in the novel deepens from an initial sign of resignation to a refrain, one that conveys not an asseveration of divine presence but an indictment of divine absence. Here is the lamentation that begins the novel's final chapter. It recalls John's beginning his *Apocalypse* with a prayer.

Robert Kennedy, whose summer home is eight miles from the home I live in all year round, was shot two nights ago. He died last night. So it goes.
Martin Luther King was shot a month ago. He died, too. So it goes.
And every day my Government gives me a count of corpses created by military science in Vietnam. So it goes.

Stately, almost monotonous, dirge-like beats confer meaning through a heightening effect. Repeated, refined, *so it goes* dazes the inner ear. It expresses the witness' bewilderment. He stands in the twenty-fifth hour devoid of belief. It comes through as *let it not be that way.* Technically, the phrase registers the narrator's switching focus to another mountain-moment, one hopefully better but actually parallel. *So it goes* is a crucial transition between those static prominences left dissociated by the story.

I compared the piecing together of these parts to the oriental serpent.

The analogy raises several implications which I want to conclude by pursuing. In the Bible the serpent marks beginnings and endings. In Genesis, the first book of the Old Testament, the serpent takes part in the drama of creation and man's fall, and then reappears in *The Revelation of John,* the last book of the New Testament, when God reverses the course of events leading to the fall by sending Michael to snare the serpent and seal it in the abyss. The biblical serpent embraces both the divine and demonic, signifying the ambivalence of cosmic creation. D. H. Lawrence, commenting on John's *Apocalypse,* relates the serpent to processes of consciousness, distinguishing between good and bad, creative liberating serpents and dark imprisoning ones. "That is, man can have the serpent with him or against him. When his serpent is with him, he is almost divine. When his serpent is against him, he is stung and envenomed and defeated from within."[4]

Slaughterhouse-Five attempts to ally humanity with the serpent in humanity's grappling with death. This "fitful duty-dance" goes back to the first human act risking death to find transcendence. Our modern reenactment takes place without hope of Michael's aid and without the help of the contemporary archangel, science. For Vonnegut, both seem feeble. The narrative convolutions of *Slaughterhouse-Five* suggest the possibility of a personal re-creation with the assistance of the bright serpent of consciousness. By directly confronting our mortality we can be alive in the present. The novel suggests several deceptions we must see through. Death is not a cartoon frame followed by facile reconstruction of dismemberment in the next frame, nor is it an entrée into a transfigured selfhood. Sentimental patriotism and science fiction prompt Billy to experience death in this fantasy way so that he will give his life in their behalf. Death is a personal end, the end. "When you're dead you're dead," Vonnegut reminds us in *Mother Night.* This truth is self-evident if we bother to think about it, but Vonnegut's point is that we are encouraged not to bother. Billy and the reader must wind through the fictions of our permanence to see what the human heart always knows: one must die one's own death.

An awareness of personal mortality places people squarely in their loneliness, from where they can openly observe who they are, how to live now. Vonnegut himself as the narrator-witness embodies this attitude. In the course of testifying to Billy's heartsickness and deadened spirit, the witness moves from a sense of personal responsibility (he will show the terror of the fire-bombing) to a sense of his own personal helplessness and disconnectedness. The testimony leads toward what the reader has sensed all along in the narrative anarchy and technical patchwork: the irrationality, the absence of successiveness, the limitation of set forms, the feebleness of the human mind, its violence, the enormity of its adversary. In the beginning the witness says that "even if wars didn't keep coming like glaciers, there would still be plain old death." At the end of the book, we are left with pictures of the countless corpse mines in Dresden. Their putrescence makes death tangible enough for the witness to breathe it in. The hyperconsciousness to language that the novel has addressed leads the reader to a deeper awareness that these are mere words, promptings toward death but not death itself. Even our linguistic constructs fall short. The novel sends us back to life.

An act of the mind in serpentine twisting is a skeptical exploration of the self's relation to the world. It leads an open, flexible course that flows with the needs of the time and the consequences of discovery, however discouraging it may be. It is life-furthering by virtue of its readiness for unpredictable directions. It knows, truth to tell, the fiction of fiction. It is an act of the mind that can double back the way God reversed the falling course of things or the way *Slaughterhouse-Five* coils its ending around to its fractured beginnings for fulfillment. Lawrence seems to be right about the divine in persons. Rudolf Bultmann explains that participation as an encounter: "God as acting does not refer to an event which can be perceived by me without myself being drawn into the event as into God's action....In other words," Bultmann continues, "to speak of God as acting involves the events of personal existence. The encounter with God can be an event for man only here and now, since man lives within the limits of space and time."[5] The novel's narrator permits the events of Billy's life to act upon him finally so that he discovers the necessity for a here and now amid the history and foretellings of doom around us. The witness in turn invites the reader's consciousness to interact with his. The rhythm of this moral interpenetration of consciousness is the form of *Slaughterhouse-Five*. The revelation that we have a present full of awareness is its good tidings.

Critics take *Slaughterhouse-Five* as a culmination in Vonnegut's career, and the assessment is valid. The novel openly treats the Allied firebombing of Dresden, which had haunted Vonnegut since he was twenty-two years old and a prisoner of war in Germany, but which he could only present in effigy in the five earlier novels.[6] His strategy, we have seen in *Slaughterhouse-Five,* is to register the mind in the act of confronting annihilation. In finding a form to tell of this disaster, Vonnegut is able to respond to the smoldering demand that this holocaust, which killed more people than did the atomic bombing of Hiroshima in 1945, not pass silently into human history, as its planners had hoped it would. Faced boldly, narrated and thereby worked through, the trauma of Dresden is exorcised of its dark spell on Vonnegut's imagination.

Vonnegut has made several public remarks which encourage us to take this breakthrough as a fulfillment of a phase in his life's work. In *Slaughterhouse-Five* itself he said that he had been working on the book all through the years he spent publishing his other books, discarding five thousand pages before settling on the one hundred and eighty-six that make up the book. He spoke freely of the entire process as "expiation,"[7] after which he was turning to the theater. Like Eliot Rosewater, Vonnegut takes leave of the work he has done so well.

7

HAPPY BIRTHDAY, WANDA JUNE and
BREAKFAST OF CHAMPIONS

> Among the tin cans, tires, rusted pipes, broken machinery,—
> One learned of the eternal. . . .
>
> Theodore Roethke, *The Far Field*

"'I'm through with novels,'" Vonnegut says in 1971, in the preface to his published play. "'I'm writing a play. It's plays from now on.'" The play he produced is *Happy Birthday, Wanda June.* In the preface to the published script from which I just quoted, Vonnegut explains the origins of the play in his being struck by Odysseus' "cruelly preposterous" behavior upon coming home. So he wrote *Penelope* as a rejoinder, and the play was presented at the Orleans Arena Theater on Cape Cod where Vonnegut and his wife were conducting the Great Books program that had occasioned the discussion of *The Odyssey. Penelope* evolved into *Happy Birthday, Wanda June,* which opened to mixed notices in New York on October 7, 1970, at the Theater de Lys, moved uptown to the Edison Theater, and closed on March 14, 1971, after 142 performances. The play's production history, however, does not convey its importance to Vonnegut. The venture was humanly crucial for him, for the company provided him with a "new family," he says in his late forties, when his own family was breaking apart as his six children grew up and went their separate ways.

Happy Birthday, Wanda June retells Odysseus' famous homecoming. Odysseus becomes Harold Ryan, age fifty, a professional soldier who has killed almost two hundred men and countless animals in various military expeditions. After eight years, Ryan, like Odysseus, comes back home unannounced. Homer's Penelope becomes Penelope Ryan, age thirty, who remains true to the legend by remaining true to her renowned husband. There are also suitors, as in the Greek story—Herb Shuttle, the vacuum cleaner salesman, and Dr. Norbert Woodley, the pacifist physician. In *The Odyssey,* Odysseus goes to elaborate lengths to hide his identity from everyone in order to test Penelope's fidelity and to display his cunning by destroying her suitors. To Homer's audience such violence is self-affirming. Prowess makes Odysseus a great seducer and a national hero, for in the ancient world cunning is what is needed to survive. Also, to the Greeks, for whom a woman is unequal to a man, Penelope is enhanced by the inordinate demands on her loyalty. Such extreme conduct makes perfect sense in its Hellenistic context. Vonnegut's finding Odysseus' behavior cruelly preposterous really encroaches on the larger issue of epic heroism and the values it extolls. His quarrel with the Greek notion of hero tells us where Vonnegut's interest lies. Whereas many writers evoke the classical past to show how puny modern man is by comparison, Vonnegut shows how its emphasis on violent destruction, carried into our crowded, contingent world, turns man into a killer and persons into worthless objects of heroic exploitation. What served Odysseus well now endangers all life. To survive now we need compassion and mercy. Dresden and Hiroshima and Vietnam are sins against life, not victories.

The warrior Harold Ryan returns home on his birthday. Only his son Paul remembers the day; and at the last minute Herb Shuttle buys a cake saying, "Happy Birthday, Wanda June," that had been left at the bakery because Wanda June was killed by an ice-cream truck while going to pick it up. It is a birthday and Harold is the honored person, but the occasion is ultimately celebrated as a day of armistice on which a new Harold is born. The two main characters, Penelope and Harold, undergo a change that expresses the new kind of values required to endure in a disintegrating world. When the play begins, Penelope breaks the bondage imposed by marriage to a hero. She appears to be a traditional wife taking her identity from her famous husband's reputation; but when that glorious absence returns home, stalking around with his killer's pride, we see that Penelope has progressed emotionally during his eight years away. She will not assent to his violence, nor does she submit to his swaggering demands. She serves as Vonnegut's polemical, independent spokeswoman for the new, ascendent moral order. Near the end of the play, she summarizes the change: "The old heroes are going to have to get used to this, Harold—the new heroes who refuse to fight. They're trying to save the planet.

There's no time for battle, no point to battle anymore." She protests against violence. She wants love somewhere in her life now. The growth in Penelope corresponds to the turn in the larger consciousness of the 1960s in America which Harold must confront. Predictably, he reacts against the new antiwar sentiment. "What kind of country has this become? The men wear beads and refuse to fight—and the women *adore* them. America's days of greatness are over." Penelope's protestations challenge Harold's chauvinism; Dr. Woodley's insults finish the job of assaulting Harold's thinking. Woodley, the healer, fusillades the killer with a discharge of verbal truths aimed at Harold's vanity: "filthy, rotten bastard," "cruel," "a living fossil," "comical." The accusation of being a despised, outmoded person when he has thought of himself as valiant cuts deepest into Harold's pride. The cause of Dr. Woodley's drunken tirade against Harold is his discovery that the mighty soldier has smashed the physician's two-hundred-year-old violin just for the thrill of witnessing its owner's reaction to loss. Harold's gesture is pathetic yet meaningful because it exemplifies a form of self-destruction which Vonnegut shows in every novel. The violin represents the cultural tradition that senseless violence is systematically decimating. Art and emotion stand defenseless against Yahooism.

When Eliot Rosewater finds himself amid the ruins of a clarinet factory in Bavaria, staring at an unarmed fireman he has just bayoneted, his mind shatters. Harold's change is more sudden, no less complete, and rendered in the same image of the clown that in the end defines Eliot. Penelope's revolt followed by Woodley's wisdom demolish Harold. Their thoughts are like poison in his head, rendering him incapable of taking his "heroic balderdash" seriously again. Actually, it is truer to the spirit of the play to say that their responses disarm him, for *Happy Birthday, Wanda June* honors the disarmament of the killer champion. The things he had been taught to believe, the country and family he thought he knew, fail Harold. Rocked by Penelope's and the country's new consciousness, he tries to kill himself but, to the chagrin of one of his victims waiting to greet him in heaven, misses. The hero of yesteryear spoils his own code of honor. The curtain falls as the champ transforms himself into a fumbling clown, which we know from the final scenes of *God Bless You, Mr. Rosewater* to be Vonnegut's tender portrait of human dignity reborn from its own vulnerability. Harold's evolution from a "vengeful ape" into a "*merciful* man" dramatizes the revolution humanity must make to survive—and to spare the planet from further bereavement. It is not overstating Vonnegut's intention to say that *Happy Birthday, Wanda June* redefines the nature of heroism for our time. It introduces the ancient idea of valor to show its danger and inadequacy. The transformation of Harold Ryan depicts the shattering of the mind-set of our age.

Vonnegut's resolution to write plays of all kinds tapered out with a ninety-minute special given on public television on March 13, 1972, called *Between Time and Timbuktu*. Subtitled "A Space Fantasy," the script anthologizes sections of Vonnegut's novels and short stories to show the scientific and zany coherence of his imagined cosmos. This experimental package taught Vonnegut that neither the stage nor the screen was his affair.

Now that we are at a divide in Vonnegut's growth that spans his achieved and experimental efforts, we can see what momentum in his art is reinforced by his turning away from fiction and then from plays. He felt strongly that writing out his war experience in *Slaughterhouse-Five* rounded out a phase in his work. The popular and critical success of the novel deepened his sense of completion. That part was over, and he wanted to move on. To catalyze a creative change in his art and life, Vonnegut looked to plays which, it appeared at the time, offered him a way out of the tightly self-involved corner he had written himself into and which plunged him into the intense relationship with the actors that a production offered. From the inwardness that has always been his range, however, we could have anticipated that Vonnegut would find plays inadequate for his moral work. In 1972 in the Preface to *Between Time and Timbuktu* he tenders his resignation from plays with the same gusto with which he turned to them—and for pretty much the same reason, namely, to evolve as artist, as he must: "I have become an enthusiast for the printed word again. I have to be that, I now understand, because I want to be a character in all of my works. I can do that in print. In a movie, somehow, the author always vanishes. Everything of mine which has been filmed so far has been one character short, and the character is me."

I I

If Vonnegut's dissatisfaction with dramatic forms brings him to articulate anew the kind of writing he is after, we do not see the concrete results in his next book, *Breakfast of Champions*. Published in 1973 when Vonnegut proclaimed a return to print, *Breakfast of Champions* had been written earlier but was held up by the author when he said that he had

stopped writing novels.[1] This novel fictionalizes the searching pronounce-
ments Vonnegut was making on the potentialities of his fiction. With
Prospero's affection, Vonnegut near the end of his tempestuous *Breakfast
of Champions* proclaims the release of "all the literary characters who have
served me so loyally" from the confines of his pages. He casts off, also,
any vestige of the realistic novel with its meaningless accumulation of details and facts. Liberation and dispersal are possible because Vonnegut
created those things; and his creation and what it imitates or represents are
the subject of *Breakfast of Champions.* Vonnegut, reflecting on his career,
addresses us and his made-up world as its ultimate creator "on a par with
the Creator of the Universe." These are preliminary ways of indicating
how the content and manner of *Breakfast of Champions* pose Vonnegut's
topic: Where do I go from here? The dilemma is taken up with a desire
to move beyond his successful formulations and with a poised, self-
accepting knowledge of the Sisyphean task behind and ahead. "This book
is my fiftieth birthday present to myself. I feel as though I am crossing
the spine of a roof—having ascended one slope."

The tale Vonnegut tells from the roof's spine is about a meeting of two
old men. One of them we know from *God Bless You, Mr. Rosewater* and
Slaughterhouse-Five; he is Kilgore Trout, the prolific visionary writer of
science fiction whose imagined worlds make him one of the greatest
prophets in the universe. But prophets are fated to be misunderstood, and
Trout is a nobody on his own planet. The other old man is Dwayne
Hoover, a Pontiac dealer whose array of properties, from "Dwayne
Hoover's Exit Eleven Pontiac Village" to a Burger Chef chain, makes Billy
Pilgrim at his commercial height appear ascetic. Dwayne Hoover "is the
hero of this book" just as he is the economic model of our culture. So
much for hero and culture. Vonnegut brings the man of property and the
man of advanced ideas together. As in the play, two mind-sets collide—
a materialistic temperament meets a visionary spirit. The result is cata-
strophic. Dwayne, who is on the brink of madness, goes berserk. Trout
gets mangled physically, as do a number of other victims of a massive
decomposition of body and mind.

The setting is Midland City, Indiana, the heart of the heart of the
country. The occasion is the cultural jamboree we enjoy mounting; this
time it is the Arts Festival celebrating the Mildred Barry Memorial Center
for the Arts in Midland City. The gathering derives from the same peace-
making spirit that made Harold Ryan's homecoming a festival of disarmament in *Happy Birthday, Wanda June,* only in *Breakfast of Champions*

the truce is on a large scale. The time is autumn, the holiday weekend of November 11, which is Veterans' Day but which Vonnegut reminds us was once "a sacred day called *Armistice Day*" because the warring nations of World War I were silent at the "eleventh minute of the eleventh hour ... [on] the eleventh day of the eleventh month." As in the play, there is a birthday—this time Vonnegut's, who was born on November 11, 1922. This locates the action in 1972 since the novel is his fiftieth birthday gift to himself.

In a book that dismisses detail as pointless, we can assume that facts of time and place create their own verisimilitude. The narrative present generates a mental excursion backward to action in 1492 and completed events in 1979 and 1981, all of which blend with the Ford Galaxies and Burger Chefs of our current moment that constitutes one indefinite past. Moreover, where the author hovers godlike over the events, his presence is likely to overtake the story. And it does. What I term the tale of *Breakfast of Champions* is its subtext. "'The big show is inside my head,'" Vonnegut says to a character for both her benefit and the reader's. Vonnegut's mind is the arts festival for which the Midland City shindig is a metaphorical expedient. Because of the deliberate doubleness of form —action as substructure overset by its creator's imagination as structure— I want to proceed first by showing the significant design of Kilgore Trout's meeting Dwayne Hoover and then by considering the pattern emerging from Vonnegut's presiding omniscience over that encounter, or the big mind show.

I I I

When Dr. Woodley announces to Harold Ryan near the finale of *Happy Birthday, Wanda June* that "the new hero will be a man of science and of peace," he informs us of the gathering importance of Kilgore Trout in Vonnegut's books. The new hero will "disarm you," Woodley predicts. *Breakfast of Champions* rounds out Trout's biography by shifting back and forth in time from the narrative focus of 1972. In 1979, two years before his death in 1981, Trout receives the Nobel Prize for Medicine for his pioneering work in mental health. At the time of the Midland City festival he is still a "nobody," disguising his amazing psychoanalytical findings in the metaphors of science fiction, which the public buys as pornography. Eliot Rosewater, the fabulously rich eccentric, recognizes

Trout's hidden genius and gets him invited to the festival. Trout lives in Cohoes, New York, and to get to Midland City he must venture west. His westward trip structures the events of the novel. It is unlike any of the legendary westward movements in American literature and history that we inevitably think of. The dangers of that fabled venture have multiplied while the rewards have been abolished. Trout's journey to the heartland is the black humorist's revision of Tocqueville's passage.

Neither the possibility of fame nor of money brings Trout out of hiding, though he is unknown and broke. He accepts the invitation to shock the false, romantic attitudes that people have about artistic life by putting in a word for failure and frustration. He will attend as "'a representative of all the thousands of artists who devoted their entire lives to a search for truth and beauty—and didn't find doodley-squat!'" he confides to Bill, the parakeet with whom he lives. When he leaves his remote sanctuary, his departure is as astonishing as Alice's falling down the rabbit-hole. Through Alice's dream, we perceive the truths about growing up amid the dishonesties of Victorian England. As Trout trudges for two days on the open road across the country, we see the wonderland of ruination that is everyday life in modern America. The virgin land of the past has become a junkyard strewn with mechanical wreckage, cars, stoves, washing machines, refrigerators, and human machines. The technological utopia promised to the statistically average person by the visionary company in *Player Piano* seems to have come to pass and been angrily dismantled by its cheated beneficiaries. Trout endures a similar rending in his travel.

In New York City Trout is mugged on Times Square, where he goes to the pornography shops to find his books, and then he is robbed and dumped, bleeding, at the Queensboro Bridge on the East River. Broke, he hitches a ride on a diesel truck named Pyramid, which conveys him across "the poisoned marshes and meadows of New Jersey" and on to Philadelphia, which greets travelers with a sign stating that it is the City of Brotherly Love "posted on the rim of a bomb crater," after which the demolished traveler arrives in the demolished state of West Virginia. Having been stripped of its coal, the land "was rearranging what was left of itself in conformity with the laws of gravity." Trout's mechanical pilgrimage on trucks ends, as we might expect, with a fatal accident, on Exit 10A outside Midland City. The "stranger in a strange land" arrives to wander more deeply through the pain that is crucifying him. Wading across Sugar Creek at the new Holiday Inn, Trout's feet become coated with a clear plastic substance that comes from a new antipersonnel bomb being manufactured at a nearby plant. The encasing of Trout's shoes and socks in plastic, so that they cannot breathe, duplicates the gradual hardening of Bokonon by *ice-nine* in *Cat's Cradle*; but as an apocalyptic image, the plastic in *Breakfast of Champions* carries the authentic stamp of our cultural trademark. We now can see the aptness of Vonnegut's setting the action in Midland City, since it recalls Midland, Michigan, home of Dow Chemical, whose creativity has found unforeseen applications for plastic. The antipersonnel bombs and napalm used against the helpless Vietnamese are Dow's notable contributions to the art of chemistry. The plastic bags for dead soldiers to which Vonnegut directs our moral attention in the book are at once emblematic of the way things are and prefigure how we end: "life is now a polymer in which the Earth is wrapped so tightly" that its energy is choked. Trout, the man of advanced ideas, shares in the fate of the Midlanders in being among the first American victims of this progressive suffocation. The next assault is Dwayne's biting off the topmost joint of Trout's right ring finger, which seems a treatable, limited brutality next to the organic violence of Midland, which is plasticizing the earth. In the novel's Epilogue, Trout meets his Creator, Kurt Vonnegut; in this final crash, Vonnegut shows off the power of his pen by throwing Trout around the solar system and then by freeing him from further artistic use.

The other party in the meeting of two lonely old men suffers a comparable disintegration. Dwayne Hoover stays at home in Midland but travels through the dilapidated places of his mind—locales as hazardous as those through which Trout passes. And both men are worked over by chemicals, though in Dwayne's case the corrosion is coming from inside. He has become a human chemical plant making harmful products. "Dwayne Hoover's body was manufacturing certain chemicals which unbalanced his mind." Dwayne seems to have grabbed and held all the money he could make on Pontiacs, Burger Chefs, and motels; and he has found no emotional gratification for his effort. Ever since his wife killed herself by drinking Drano, he has never wanted to hear love mentioned again; and yet with his lover Francine he wanted to be loved "for his body and soul, not for what his money could buy." Like Billy Pilgrim before him, Dwayne is in hopeless conflict because he knows that love makes life dangerous, even deadly, but also makes life possible. His affliction is a sense of loneliness that he feels powerless to get away from. "'I've lost my way,'" he acknowledges to Francine. "'I need somebody to take me by the hand and lead me out of the woods.'" Francine, herself shy about love ever since her husband was shipped home from Vietnam in a plastic body bag, suggests that the arriving artists might help; so Dwayne looks to the Festival for whatever guidance art and artists might provide. Dwayne never escapes from his loneliness. He needs and seeks human contact but spends the Veterans' Day weekend intensifying his isolation by assaulting the people around him. This Armistice holiday is Dwayne's call to arms against the enemy, life. He begins with insults and a little homey shoot-out, smashing the fixtures in his toilet. Then, in his vacant parking lot, where he placed hope for self-esteem, he experiences a radical displacement from the home town he knows so well. "'Where am I?'" he muses placidly while seated in his used Plymouth Fury. He is amid the junk of his ambition, which are the worn-out props of his sanity. Going to his Pontiac showroom is not likely to help him regain an equilibrium since even a stable person is likely to be unsettled by the Hawaiian Week decor around the place as a sales promotion—green plastic sheets simulating leaves over a sawed-off telephone pole to evoke Aloha. Harry Le Sabre, the car salesman in "lettuce-green leotard, straw sandals, a grass skirt, and a pink T-shirt" does not instill confidence in the actual. When Dwayne meets Trout at the Holiday Inn, he does get a truth about the world that is a fresh viewpoint, but the truth does not save him. Snatching Trout's *Now It Can Be Told,* Dwayne reads that we are all robots. Like all of the revealed secrets scattered throughout Vonnegut's novels, Trout's saving message comes clothed in irony. *Now It Can Be Told* addresses its reader as one chosen by the Creator of the Universe to be "'the only creature in the entire Universe who has free will.'" Such a person is exempt from the limitation imposed on others in order to conduct an experiment in freedom. Other persons may be regarded as mechanical objects in service of this autonomous person's task of figuring out "'what to do next.'" Trout's revelation describes the underlying arrogance of our behavior. Dwayne proceeds to act out Trout's sardonic authorization and goes on a rampage of destruction, which, like the society that conditioned Dwayne, enacts his own orgy of masochism. He is left friendless and destitute by the lawsuits filed by his victims.

In a universe where every substance is defined by its function in some experiment—"loving machines, hating machines . . . truthful machines, lying machines"—creatures do not encounter one another. Persons *meet;* robots and forces collide. The form of the tale of Trout's impact on Dwayne is that of collision. Collision in *Breakfast of Champions* is the unifying principle derived from a natural law of Vonnegut's cosmos.

Continents, we are told, ride a slab that drifts precariously "on molten glurp"; and "when one slab crashed into another one, mountains were made." A violent crashing is continually "going on" in the universe, leading scientists to predict "that ice ages would continue to occur." Like world, like people. Nations grind against one another; creatures strike one another. We are "doomed to collide and collide and collide." Collision is the secret knowledge behind the revelations in *Now It Can Be Told*, which implies that God moves not only in mysterious ways but also in disastrous ways. "'You ever see one of His volcanoes or tornadoes or tidal waves? Anybody ever tell you about the Ice Ages He arranges for every half-million years?'" asks Trout of the trucker taking him across the blighted Jersey meadows. Dwayne comes to the same insight from his personal experience. He comes to think of the test cars, which Pontiac scientists destroy to discover their breaking point, as the paradigm for all life. The GM research lab occasions Dwayne's momentous insight into life: "'I couldn't help wondering if that was what God put me on Earth for—to find out how much a man could take without breaking.'" Where Alice's adventures in wonderland dramatize the irregularity of the process of growing up, Trout's and Dwayne's adventures in our wonderland of the actual show the suffering and unintelligibility of daily living.

Vonnegut's emphasis on boundless suffering explains why he places a passage from the Book of Job as the novel's epigraph to shade our reading of Trout's clash with Dwayne. The Book of Job tells of a blameless holy man who is tried by God to the point of superhuman suffering. To prove to Satan that there is a person who is steadfastly faithful, God allows Satan to try Job. Job loses all his worldly possessions; he loses his children; he breaks out in hideous sores; and he remains true to God. But Job does lament, and he does ask God to explain why he meted out such trials. The Lord ignores Job's questions, in the same way that he did not explain his change of plans to destroy Nineveh to his prophet Jonah. The Lord will only affirm his wisdom, leaving Job to accept that unfathomable wisdom with a faith that goes beyond answers. Job is capable of such a faith, but his affirming humility before God's inscrutability reveals a still deeper crisis than that of physical suffering. Job stands in a vacuum of belief in which anything that faith could say about God is inadequate. His lament is also for the loss of his trust in his ability to live outside of a relationship with God; and with God remaining hidden and with his disregard for Job's questions, that relationship has been undermined.

Breakfast of Champions confronts its reader with a comparable over-whelming question about the meaning of and in the universe. How do you account for evil in a world for which there is a god? The novel raises complaints about suffering, especially innocent suffering such as Job's, within a moral context of deeply shaken faith. As *Cat's Cradle* reiterates the prophetic warning of the Book of Jonah without its promise of deliverance, *Breakfast of Champions* invokes the skepticism of the Book of Job without offering its consolation of faith. Job has confronted God, and that encounter indicates his presence in the universe. Job can live life with a sign of the providence that sustains creation. Where is the reassuring splendor of creation in *Breakfast of Champions?* How is the universe maintained? Job can adore what he cannot comprehend, but that adoration is inadequate to deal with the disintegrating universe Vonnegut constructs. For persons to survive with faith, and for creation itself not to be violently blotted out, seem against the law of nature. Life now proceeds not by grace or reason but by a will-o'-the-wisp that heaves force against disruptive force. Like life, like novel—*Breakfast of Champions* patterns the tale of a meeting of two lonely old men according to the universal scheme of collision.

I V

The destructive impact of Trout on Dwayne poses the novel's theme in structural terms: How do we respond to the inevitable collisions that make up our lives? The possible responses are obviously limited. Any attempt in the book to check disaster ends up hastening it. The agonized lives of the characters warn against such action, pursuit of money or science yield illusions of control over our lives. Passivity would seem less perilous. One can withdraw and hope, as Trout does, to spend one's days without touching another human again; but even Trout is lured out of his solitude to spread the very insight (that we are machines) that drove him there, and then he is caught in the pile-up. Again, our attempts to master the mysterious activity of the world finally implicate us further in its turmoil. In his bewilderment, Vonnegut speculates on how the deity responds to upheavals in his creation. He "'wasn't any conservationist,'" as Trout theologizes. Once the volcanoes erupt and the tornadoes swirl, God sits back to be entertained by the fireworks. Vonnegut takes his cue from the Creator, the eternal black humorist. "For want of anything better to do, we became fans of collisions." The spectator's stance produces the peculiarly humorous wisdom documents recurring in the novels: Jonah in *Cat's Cradle* gives us his record of human stupidity; Eliot Rosewater's *Domesday Book* presents in apple-pie order a ledger of his philanthropic operations during the apocalypse; Trout tells it as it is in *Now It Can Be Told*; and to this imaginary library of visionary documents, Vonnegut makes a personal contribution of a notebook of a cosmic fan. The superstructure of *Breakfast of Champions* is that of an archeological scrapbook composed of wise precepts for life on a planet that was, Earth.

At the time that Trout's message sends Dwayne over the brink of sanity, the planet too is on the verge of extinction. By 1972 industrial greed has been systematically destroying Earth's resources. Vonnegut, seeing this profiteering as the shaping spirit of American history, gives a revised account of the story of our past to show how universal destruction fulfills the rapacity hiding within the American search for prosperity and pursuit of happiness. It is the black humorist's guide to American history. In 1492 sea pirates cheated and robbed the natives until they were strong enough to found a government which, in the name of freedom, sanctioned the making of black persons into black machines for the economic good of white farmers. Then the land was laid waste under the guise of expansion. In the course of events, presidents were intermittently shot when the frenetic populace stopped their tearing around long enough to take aim. In fine, America's story is one of affluent murder and suicide; and we can see that Dwayne Hoover is its native son, the embodiment of that grand, forgotten political experiment known as the U. S. A., "a country which was called *America* for short."

Vonnegut writes of Earth the way Jonah writes of San Lorenzo in *Cat's Cradle*: as the survivor who recalls what it was like before it disintegrated. He exhumes the bric-a-brac of our current everyday life, which are by this time of Vonnegut's writing—or in the time zone of his heart from which he is writing—so unfamiliar that he draws them for us with a felt-tip pen. The novel is dotted with illustrations of the apple, the pea, the lamb, the chicken, the hamburger, the Christmas card, the mailbox, and naturally the welcome sign of the Holiday Inn for the weary interstate traveler. In *Slaughterhouse-Five* illustrations were part of Vonnegut's overall formal experimentation, but in *Breakfast of Champions* they are poignant reminders of loss. By drawing the fruits and wares of our daily life as though they were the dinosaurs, he brings us to confront the fatal consequences of our ignominy: we are faced with, as an accomplished fact, the oblivion we are making. Our actions, furthermore, are destroying our feelings. The fleets of Plymouth Fury, Oldsmobile Tornado, Chevrolet Caprice, and Pontiac Ventura tooling around the country show by their names that the venerated machine has appropriated our emotional energy. Vonnegut sees the remote days of 1972 as the time when the human species went out on an evolutionary limb, and he diagnoses two symptoms accompanying the terminal state. Emotional entropy is one sign. Satisfied that Plymouth express their fury and Chevrolet their caprice, "most mammals were senile or dead by the time they were seventeen." Motel lobbies and car showrooms are where the anthropoids find exotic geography, and they take their identities from television shows. They are blind to the natural world and are unable to express their feelings. Where there is no emotion, no culture can thrive, and absence of culture is the second indication that the species is dying out. Culture, as we saw in *Player Piano*, is humanity's way of adapting to the environment; it is our essential ecology, for culture puts us at the conscious center of the universe. In a 1973 interview Vonnegut says that the American experience has been an unhappy one in large part because of our "living without a culture."[2] His complaint is echoed in the Preface to *Breakfast of Champions*: "I have no culture, no humane harmony in my brains. I can't live without a culture anymore." His lament heightens the significance of the cancellation of the Midland City Arts Festival because of Dwayne's madness. Ragtag as the artists are, they offer some hope through their search for expressiveness. Their art is necessary for our survival.

The humane harmony Vonnegut needs does come about. In an earlier novel, Eliot Rosewater scatters his money around to achieve a momentary balance; now Vonnegut proceeds to discard áll the cultural rubbish that has accumulated in his mind over fifty years. The big show in his head is an act of dispossession of the values emerging from life as represented by Midland City. By discarding the cultural myths through which malice and greed denigrate persons and natural riches into objects of abuse, Vonnegut suspends hostilities between himself and the world. This emotional cessation honors his private Armistice Day and is his fiftieth birthday gift to himself.

Vonnegut wants to toss out junk in order to retain only "sacred things." His reason for going to Midland City is "to be born again." He is not reborn but he relearns that forces in our souls prevent transformation. Again collision images the spiritual turmoil that awaits us. "One force had a sudden advantage over another, and spiritual continents began to shrug and heave." The sacred, then, resides neither in himself nor in any individual human being. Robo Karabekian, a trashy minimalist painter who has been invited to the Festival, brings Vonnegut to his fullest understanding of the sacred: "'Our awareness is all that is alive and maybe sacred in any of us.'" Karabekian calls our awareness a band of light, which describes his kind of painting. The bogus painter-philosopher defines for Vonnegut, the doodler-novelist, what is sacred. Awareness is all that the fan of collision can hope to attain and awareness depends on collective, interpenetration of mind. Vonnegut writes from that band of unwavering light in himself, addressing the band at the core "of each person who reads this book," and thereby he furthers the collectivity of the sacred.

What I said about the design of *Slaughterhouse-Five* helps us to understand how this awareness shapes its companion book. The form of *Breakfast of Champions* is an act of the mind reflecting on our self-inflicted oblivion which Vonnegut sees as imminent. The unwavering band of light is what remains when all the artifacts and human connections are extinguished, as they are for the mortally lonely narrator, Kurt Vonnegut. This final light illumines his grief. He becomes an instrument extending the line of perceptivity that is required for awareness to deepen into compassion. The movement from the Preface to the Epilogue marks this illumination. The Preface begins the book dogmatically, with Vonnegut denouncing the refuse that clutters his mind and flaunting his impoliteness. Twenty-four chapters follow, like so many hours of our day, filled with our quotidian disasters. The Epilogue lifts us out of time into the twenty-fifth hour of Vonnegut's consciousness. The novel comes to a close with a post-apocalyptic gesture of humility as he frees his characters, ending the novel with a portrait of sorrow. The last page has no words; we move from word to picture, or from idea to feeling. Facing us is a self-portrait of Vonnegut weeping, in profile. We are brought beyond words to silence.

This silence goes back to the unexpected hush that fell in 1918 when at the eleventh minute of the eleventh hour on the eleventh day of the eleventh month—Armistice Day—nations ceased fighting. Old men told Vonnegut that the moment of "sudden silence was the Voice of God." God speaks through silence in generations when his word falls on completely deaf ears. Vonnegut in the book expresses a keen interest about what God would have to say about all the collisions going on. Vonnegut even plays God in the oldest of artistic guises, the omniscient Creator of his fictions, just to see if the giving and the taking of fictional life provides an insight into God's knowledge. How can he, as a second Creator of the world, transform reality back into its potentialities and so escape its chaos? Vonnegut's intrusion into the text, scaffolding an overstructure of reflection, is not a gimmick but an act of love. The final silence evoked by his self-portrait resonates with the recognition of the Creator's failure to comprehend and to save his world. We are told in Isaiah 40:8 that "the word of our God stands forever." His word does so in the sacred permanence of silence, to which Vonnegut adds his enduring lament that gives serenity in the hope for some future explanation breaking through this divine silence.

8

SLAPSTICK

> The fundamental joke with Laurel and Hardy, it seems to me, was that they did their best with every test.
> They never failed to bargain in good faith with their destinies, and were screamingly adorable and funny on that account.
>
> Vonnegut, *Slapstick*

At the end of a Laurel and Hardy film comedy, the camera usually fades out on the two battered but undaunted partners being endlessly chased by destiny, often in the form of a furious cop or a hapless victim. Whether in a getaway car that seems to be crushed beyond use or staggering and stumbling on their feet because they have been stretched and shrunk by torture, the two dreadnoughts still go on. The closing effect of such slapstick of pursuit becomes the opening gesture of Vonnegut's *Slapstick*. The novel fades in on Kurt Vonnegut and his brother Bernard, steadfast sharers in family misfortune, in their own unresolved race with destiny flying to their favorite Uncle Alex's funeral in Indianapolis.

Death and destiny have been Vonnegut's subjects since he began writing. His work thus far has been a novel-by-novel exploration of the distressful moment near life's end, which, as we have seen, contains for Vonnegut's characters an experience of the end of the world. His stories describe the effects of catastrophe on the planet, voice the pain felt in the minds and hearts of victims, and rail against the agencies of disaster; but the stories always fall short of offering any explanation for it all. The dazed bewilderment over the massive collisions with which *Breakfast of Champions,* his previous novel, ends remains unsolved in Vonnegut's subsequent and most recent book, *Slapstick: or Lonesome No More! Slapstick* describes a world laid waste by natural and human destructiveness without even modestly proposing a reason or a corrective for it. This, his eighth novel, deepens Vonnegut's reflection on the horror of a nation's perishing. Where *Breakfast of Champions* contrives a history of America to coincide with the cruelty of current life, *Slapstick,* Vonnegut's 1976 book, implicitly contributes to the country's 200th birthday party by celebrating its requiem.

Without essentially altering his established material or practiced style, Vonnegut advances his art in *Slapstick* through tone. Doom is handled quietly, philosophically, in the way that Laurel and Hardy throw pies with thoughtful poise. The novel's dramatic action revolves around cruelty and turmoil, yet it reaches across a long emotional distance that removes any trace of bitterness or sentimentality. And like Stan and Ollie, Vonnegut plays himself in *Slapstick.* He becomes the character in this work that he said in his Preface to *Between Time and Timbuktu* he wanted to be— and was encouraged to be, I believe, by *A Time To Die,* Tom Wicker's moving account of how the Attica uprising of 1971 caused him to redirect the entire course of his life. Vonnegut now uses fiction to achieve just such a personal transformation of his writing. All the Alicelike trips through wonderland that comprise the new novel are falls down the rabbit holes of his mind, wending through the remote passages of his childhood to emerge in the channel of his creative achievement. *Slapstick* is deliberately a spiritual autobiography, an act of Vonnegut's mind, logging his responses to the disquieting origins of his creativeness. The fictionalized memoir is not nearly as melancholy an account as Vonnegut found Wicker's to be. Vonnegut looks back from the long perspective of very old age, which can see the human comedy in the trappings of utter defeat.

The novel begins with a prologue introducing the story proper and detailing certain facts of Vonnegut's life that dispose him to dwell on "desolated cities and spiritual cannibalism and incest and loneliness and lovelessness and death, and so on." As a child, Kurt, his older brother Bernard, and his sister Alice were part of a large, extended family with strong ties to Indianapolis as well as deep cultural loyalties to their German origins. During World War I, the family's capacity for self-respect was stamped out by the hatred for things German that overtook America. Consequently, Kurt, Bernard, and Alice were raised without the humanizing awareness of their rich European heritage. After the subsequent hardships of the Great Depression and World War II, the family entirely lost its spirit. That loss of vitality left the three children with a permanent feeling of displacement. "We didn't belong anywhere in particular any more. We were interchangeable parts in the American machine." There was, nevertheless, good feeling among the three and their Uncle Alex, whose funeral prompts Kurt Vonnegut to look back on his life. There were also instances of insanity in the family. And there was death. Alice's death from cancer at the age of 41 had the greatest impact on Vonnegut, who was left with three of her four sons to raise and with the enduring gift of her imagination. Everything Vonnegut has written is addressed to her. "She was the secret of whatever artistic unity I had ever achieved. She was the secret of my technique." Their shared mental life as children provides the material for the main theme of *Slapstick*. "It depicts myself and my beautiful sister as monsters, and so on." In her final hour, Alice communicated in a single word a possible way to face the odds of life. "'Slapstick,'" she said to her brothers.

While in flight to Uncle Alex's funeral, Vonnegut daydreams about a centenarian, Dr. Wilbur Daffodil-11 Swain. Wilbur bears a notable resemblance to Louis-Ferdinand Céline, the French physician-writer whose "duty-dance with death" informs *Slaughterhouse-Five*. In a 1975 Introduction to the Penguin edition of Céline's *Rigadoon*, Vonnegut spells out for us his fascination with one of the grimmest novelists of this century. Vonnegut is drawn to Céline's impoliteness, his self-mockery, his choosing to be a healer, to the poor, and his obsession with catastrophes. When World War II was ending, Céline went straight to Berlin, which was the center of the destruction. Wilbur Daffodil-11 Swain, like both Céline and Vonnegut, is writing a memoir that involves the total collapse of civilization. The stylistic and moral influence Céline exerts on Vonnegut's work is so strong that *Slapstick* comes across as an abbreviated *Journey to the End of the Night,* during which Wilbur visualizes death on the American installment plan.

Vonnegut's remembered past refracted in Wilbur's bizarre history comprises *Slapstick*. Taken together, Vonnegut and his double, Wilbur, are soulmates—a spiritual Stan and Ollie absorbing comparable blows from an absurd, eccentric universe, about which they share cosmic, self-mocking gags.

Wilbur's curious full name tells us that he comes from a special time and place. The war waged by the bandit King of Michigan against the

Great Lake pirates and the Duke of Oklahoma has been settled by Wilbur, who, acting through his power as President of the United States of America, has resold the Louisana Purchase to the Michigan king. The armistice is an uneasy suspension of hostilities, however, because Wilbur lives in the huge wake of other devastations. The Albanian flu, Tourette's Disease (which makes people involuntarily utter obscenities), and other natural plagues have decimated the population. Humanity has added to the mess with pathogenic habits of its own, such as spreading Idiot's Delight by using money as power, shrinking people with the Green Death to curtail food consumption, polluting the planet (by the time of the novel, a relatively benign pastime), and infecting one another with loneliness, the most virulent organism around.

Wilbur's home is the junk-filled lobby of the Empire State Building, where he beds down on heaps of old rags. The elevator shaft serves as the toilet. He inhabits the Island of Death—once known as Manhattan, now a post-apocalyptic ailanthus jungle dubbed Skyscraper National Park. Wilbur's nearest neighbor is Vera Chipmunk-5 Zappa, who lives in a pastoral retreat on the Island along the shores of the East River, where slaves raise animals and food. In a place where havoc is the only order, death the measure of change, and slavery the desired mode of living, we are not surprised to find that the chief constructive effort is expended on building a pyramid, because pyramids commemorate death through the labor of human bondage. On the site of what used to be Times Square, "an amorphous trash-pile" is growing into a structure that "will clearly be a pyramid."

If horror describes Wilbur's condition, the nightmare outlines his lifestory. He and his fraternal twin Eliza are born disfigured, with six fingers on each hand, six toes on each foot, four nipples, and "the features of adult, fossil human beings . . . massive brow-ridges, sloping foreheads, and steamshovel jaws." Their embarrassed millionaire parents seclude the children in Vermont, where Wilbur and Eliza become the monsters society already assumed that they were. To compensate for the absence of warm feelings around them, the twins develop a symbiotic genius and function perfectly as one complete, developing being. Eliza handles the intuitive side; Wilbur, the deductive.

At 15 they are separated. Wilbur, having inadvertently revealed his intelligence, is sent off to school and eventually to Harvard to study medicine. The division of Wilbur's and Eliza's wonderful joint wholeness is mortal. "The two happiest children that history has so far known" become among the most miserable. Eliza gets sent to an institution for "her sort," falls victim to the shyster lawyer Norman Mushari, Jr., whose legal preying on the rich we know well from *God Bless You, Mr. Rosewater*, moves to Peru, materializes in Boston long enough to accuse Wilbur of treating her like "'some kind of tumor that had to be removed from your side,'" and dies on Mars. Cut off from mental intimacy with her brother, Eliza turns into "little more than a human vegetable."

Wilbur also devolves, but in a way that we define as the American road to success. He becomes a pediatrician to take care of the kinds of needs left unattended in his own childhood. Wilbur subsequently becomes a senator and then president, as befits the scion of a great American family. (Wilbur's lineage includes the Mellons, the Vanderbilts, and the Rockefellers.) As president—the last one of the nation, as it turns out—Wilbur institutes a social scheme of artificially extended families that he and Eliza worked out long ago. There will be the Daffodils, the Chipmunks, the Orioles, the Uraniums, and other such totemic networks to guarantee a sense of belonging for all persons. This program was the crux of Wilbur's campaign promise, "Lonesome No More!" His idealistic plan is the newest of the countless visionary projects proposed in Vonnegut's novels that cannot succeed: EPICAC XIV does not computerize the nation into uniform contentment; Winston Niles Rumfoord's Church of the God of the Utterly Indifferent does not make spiritual sense of a strange universe; Bokonon's San Lorenzo does not relieve human suffering; Eliot Rosewater's philanthropy merely drives him insane—and so it goes. Wilbur Daffodil-11 Swain's government-issued names do not bring all the isolated Americans together. America is already suffering too greatly from a fulminatory case of the loneliness virus. To cope with his depression over the failure of his new humane laws, Wilbur takes to drugs, notably tribenzo-Deportamil. Ever-increasing dosages detach him from the vast ills that he cannot cure. After his 101st birthday, senile and addicted, Wilbur dies on the Island of Death. Like birth, longevity has been a burden for Wilbur. He spent his many years assuming the duties of survivorship, futilely picking up the pieces of a world that could never come together again.

Understandably, Wilbur comes to relate to himself as dead, "a brother to skeletons," before the fact. The pyramid being built at Broadway and 42nd Street reflects the inner lifelessness Wilbur has felt for his far too many years on Earth among the living and the other dead. Wilbur, a pharaoh of modern civilization, will find within the tomb's masonry the oddments of his life—"oil drums and tires and automobile parts and office furniture and theater seats, too, and all manner of junk." Underneath this stuff lies the secret to *Slapstick*. "Its meaning, which is minuscule in any event, lies beneath the manhole cover over which the pyramid is constructed. It is the body of a stillborn male."

If Wilbur's memoir is a testament of "a life that was never lived," then we can see why he chooses the art of writing to express his unlived life: words can give his profound sense of loss a communicable shape. At the end of *Cat's Cradle,* the dying, wizened Bokonon advises Jonah to write a history of all the stupidity that he has witnessed. Wilbur acts as a Jonah to his own Bokonon, his fictive predecessor of utopian rule. In writing from his inner emptiness, Wilbur becomes another of Vonnegut's survivor-narrators—his Ishmaels of the spirit—who serve as archaeologists of a civilization and a personal life that are disintegrating.

II

Inspired by Alice's deathbed utterance, Vonnegut gives his customarily plain tale a special cast by borrowing from the genius of early American screen comedy. "I have called it 'Slapstick' because it is grotesque, situational poetry—like the slapstick film comedies, especially those of Laurel and Hardy, of long ago." Where recently in *Ragtime,* for example, E. L. Doctorow draws on a period manner to establish a historical dialectic correspondence between then and now, Vonnegut uses a popular form remembered from childhood to show its timeless expression of the endurance through disaster that is his life. We have seen before how Vonnegut borrows from our popular culture—the space odyssey, the whodunit, the romance, the horror film, or graffiti—to mold a new novelistic shape. Vonnegut's talent comes through most effectively when he lifts a simple story with an explicit moral (which he often states for us) from a known genre and then satirizes his use of it. The result is a parody narrative in which Vonnegut does not imitate human action but imitates another imitation.

Vonnegut understands well that screen low-comedy presents the audience with a poem through a series of gestures. Continuity of action counts for much less in slapstick film than does gesture. Such comedy coheres through spare ritual conduct—stupidity creating catastrophe, dumb, ill-judged violence bringing about destruction in images that we can all grasp immediately.

In the novel itself, Vonnegut states his fondness for Laurel and Hardy: "They never failed to bargain in good faith with their destinies, and were screamingly adorable and funny on that account." Vonnegut does not cite a specific Laurel and Hardy film, but their masterpiece, *The Music Box* (1932), which brought them an Oscar, catches the deal they make with fate. The two are delivering an electric piano to a house on the top of an incredible hill. They naturally take the difficult route up a steep flight of steps, and have to haul the piano up the steps several times due to blunders. After repeated, arduous entries into the house, the clumsy pair destroy the furnishings trying to position the piano. Finally, their Sisyphean job ends. Dressed nattily in bowler hats, overalls, white shirts, and ties, Stan and Ollie stand with self-acceptance amid their botch. Ollie says to the stunned owners of the house, "Service with a smile." They personify human dignity born of its own ineptitude. *Slapstick* is peopled by the blundering idiots and scurvy knaves of that zany world, and their perpetual blundering explains that our humanity is bound up with imperfection. This sympathy for human shortcomings leads Vonnegut to plead for simple kindness. Gentle decency, far more than idealistic theories, is needed for us to live with our salutary imperfections.

God Bless You, Mr. Rosewater prefigures Vonnegut's fuller use of screen comedy when he pictures Eliot during his breakdown as a "Chaplinesque *boulevardier.*" Here now is the opening shot of Wilbur in *Slapstick:*

> There is a small clearing in the jungle. A blue-eyed, lantern-jawed old white man, who is two meters tall and one hundred years old, sits in the clearing on what was once the back seat of a taxicab.

A grandee of the apocalypse sits on a fragment throne as though taken from an old studio set of a vanished city. His effort to acknowledge the surrounding havoc is expressed merely by how he sits—by an attitude—rather than by what action he takes.

Laurel and Hardy and Chaplin also provide Vonnegut with a way to unify his introspective folktale. They are masters of inflection. Their comedy develops as they carefully shade their physical stance and emotional attitude toward the gag. In *Slapstick* Vonnegut proceeds by modulating his numerous attitudes toward the jungle of extinction. *Slapstick* is a sequence of mental positions without a climax. A minimal story line is ornamented with dialogue and situation. The effect is that of improvisation supporting an unobtrusive plan. Wilbur's chronological recollection of his life is the story's binding thread, which Vonnegut fastens to his personal prologue and epilogue. Vonnegut as usual delights in acknowledging "all the loose ends of the yarn" while composing in strip-cartoon layout a series of gallows gags that blend, in a carefully paced tempo, outlandish behavior with a feeling of inevitability.

The form of *Slapstick* embodies a metamorphosis from the imperfect wholeness of childhood to the breakup of senility. The only advice Wilbur offers about dealing with this change is a passage from Jesus' Sermon on the Mount. "'Take no thought for the morrow,'" he tells Vera, who is concerned about what will happen to her slaves when she dies, "'for the morrow shall take thought for the things of itself. Sufficient unto the day is the evil thereof.'" We are invited to become like children again during times of suffering and trust that life will father us. God's care and bound-less goodness will absorb the evil of the day. The pain is still there, but this simple trust makes it hurt less and makes it possible to go on.

The ending of *Slapstick* underlines Wilbur's moral injunction to become spiritual children through the image of Melody, Wilbur's "illiterate, rickety, pregnant little granddaughter" of 16, who is making her way eastward from Michigan to New York "in search of her legendary grand-father." One immediately thinks of that other slapstick queen of modern fiction, Lena Grove in Faulkner's *Light in August.* Lena's and Melody's tramplike innocence brings many people to their aid. Melody, Vonnegut says, "is what I feel to be, when I experiment with old age, all that is left of my optimistic imagination, of my creativeness." Once again, Vonnegut comes around to affirming art as a holding action against the onslaught of meaninglessness.

The devolving course of Wilbur's and Vonnegut's combined mental process returns to the preoccupation of the contemporary mind with the holocaust. In the moral background of the novel are the atomic bomb and the killing of 100 million people in this century's wars and death camps. These events shape *Slapstick* as well as modern history. *Slapstick* is Vonne-gut's meditative documentary—his sorrow and pity in low-comedy form—about how we live now in the aftermath of the holocaust. During such a crisis, human beings require a sense of continuity and relatedness to what comes before and after life. We find that struggle to achieve a new rela-tionship with the world expressed in *Slapstick* through the image of the survivor as creator. Creativeness, like Wilbur's happy childhood, takes two forms. The external formulation of the struggle for meaning is the novel itself. The inner, spiritual mode generating the story is rendered through Melody. Simply to go on, as Melody does, taking things as they come, is to know how to live with suffering; and when everything falls apart, to pick up and begin again with clownish joyousness from the act of doing so is all there is to do. We learn by feeling. Such purity of heart is the beginning of unity within one's spirit.

EPILOGUE

> In plain words, Chaos is the law of nature;
> Order was the dream of man.
> Henry Adams, *The Education of Henry Adams*

It is always hazardous to attempt to sum up an artist's achievement. When the artist is at the high tide of his creative energy, as Vonnegut is at the moment, the time is especially inopportune. I do not intend here impertinently to wrap up what Vonnegut's art is all about or to establish his place in American fiction. Nor would I risk forecasting the direction that the art might take of a writer on the cutting edge of fiction who has made a specialty of formal iconoclasm and stylistic impoliteness. But I would like to extend my readings of the individual novelistic forms by putting in a concluding, but by no means conclusive, word about the distinctive quality of mind that emerges from the stories Vonnegut composes. Quality of mind is, after all, the soul of fiction. Character and plot are but expedients through which the writer transmits his sensitivity of mind.

From a broad perspective, Vonnegut's career shows a gradual personalization of story. The simple shifts in point of view reveal this pattern. In *Player Piano* and *The Sirens of Titan*, his first two novels, the teller is a detached narrator. Then, in *Mother Night* and *Cat's Cradle*, there are dissembled first-person narrators who partake in the action while retaining a separateness from Vonnegut himself. With *God Bless You, Mr. Rosewater,* the lamentation of *Mother Night* and the satire of *Cat's Cradle* deriving from those personae are relaxed into the sympathetic tenderness born of a caring, affirming teller. But though there is warmth in the rendering of Eliot Rosewater's scheme to love everybody, there is also distance. With most authors this aesthetic distance is part of the indirection that is fiction-making. By making an issue of discarding his masks in *Slaughterhouse-Five*, however, Vonnegut invites us to consider the earlier narrators as tellers manqué. Their inadequacy for the kind of self-investigative fiction Vonnegut strives for is emphasized by his self-conscious stepping into the action of *Breakfast of Champions*. He makes explicit his purpose in violating the convention of masking the narrator: he goes to the Midland City Arts Festival "to be born again." "I, the author, am suddenly transformed by what I have done so far," he confesses. *Slapstick*, his most recent novel, enlarges Vonnegut's presence in his writing by composing a spiritual autobiography.

The transformation of his narrative posture, then, tells us the transformation his art is to bring about. We can put it this way: the narrator, who is baring his heart, allows Vonnegut to address himself as well as addressing us. The use of the narrator openly registering his inner convictions about the story has brought Vonnegut to write his strongest fiction. Such a narrator is his subjective correlative.

This technical refinement would not bear noting if it did not derive from deep changes in Vonnegut's thinking about his art. The narrative masks, we saw, move the writer from observer of disaster to participant in it; and by continually correcting his point of view, Vonnegut redefines the aim of his fiction from social critique to self-exploration. Fiction eventually brings Vonnegut to know himself in relation to the world he imagines, thereby fusing storytelling with self-creation. (Were we at this point to place his critical essays alongside his fictions, we could see Vonnegut's growing insistence on writing as carrying the moral imperative of personal responsibility.) In the books up to *Slaughterhouse-Five* the protagonists are humanized through a knowledge of suffering. As narrator-protagonist of *Slaughterhouse-Five*, Vonnegut is schooled in the duty of art by acquiring a compassionate view of experience. As the narrator who plays Creator of the (fictive) Universe in *Breakfast of Champions*, and as the survivor-physician who turns memoirist in *Slapstick*, he learns the deep wisdom of Job and Jonah that God's plan is inscrutable and defies human comprehension—or, put in secular terms, that order is but a dream, a human fantasy that cannot modify the chaos which rules nature. Out of a sense of helplessness before cosmic anarchy, Vonnegut turns to the formative power of art to restore himself. Paradoxically, the

the source of distressing news—his novels—embraces Vonnegut's self-creation. Fiction, in the end, for Vonnegut must go beyond instructing readers to transforming its creator. In the Dresden novel he commits himself to himself by making his peace with the massacre that defied speech yet demanded a literate response. In the Midland City novel he commits himself to the world in all its sacred accidentalness, and this tentative affirmation balances the abiding tension in his novels between self and universe.

There is a story about the power of stories within *Cat's Cradle* that capsulizes the lesson Vonnegut learns in the course of writing his books. It centers on Dr. Felix Hoenikker, the renowned scientist from the Research Lab in Ilium, New York. Dr. Hoenikker shared in the creation of the atomic bomb and single-handedly discovered the direful *ice-nine* that finishes the disastrous shattering of the world, which was begun by the atomic bomb. For all of his intellectual curiosity, he never read "'a novel or even a short story,'" as far as his fubsy but imaginative son, Newt, can recall. He should have. Without literature, as Julian Castle from the same novel reminds us, a person dies either of "'putresence of the heart or atrophy of the nervous system.'" Dr. Hoenikker died of both.

For Vonnegut, fiction serves the great moral purpose of breathing life back into life. Books are restorative, especially if they train readers to be cosmic fans. So in dark times he uses the therapy of laughter to evoke the brightness that is concealed by fear. Because the times are deceitful, he satirizes their false claims. Because we are caught in spiritual tyranny, he celebrates the liberating power of the imagination. Vonnegut wants to reveal what Blake called "the infinite which was hid" so that we can with new energy transform the nowhere of all the mental San Lorenzos we have made for ourselves into the now-here of love.

In such a place of the heart, love and power would unite to allow the compassionate real self to emerge from the secrecy it adopts for survival. Feeling and action could then be one. Such is the case with Melody, Wilbur's granddaughter in *Slapstick*. Vonnegut attempts through his novels to sensitize his readers to the need for reversing the way the politics of power have infiltrated the intimacies of experience. If we turn round Dwayne Hoover's discovery, we can see how this revolution might begin. Where Dwayne Hoover learns that human creatures are robots, we are to perceive the person behind the human machine. Vonnegut implies through the masses of automatons in his fiction that most people, following the code of the technological system they live in, fail to recognize the humanness in others and, therefore, in themselves. His novels bear witness to the rareness and the danger of recognizing others in open affection. Paul Proteus can no longer fit into his society; Howard Campbell prefers to kill himself rather than live with the newly aroused idea that he is a feeling person responsible to others; Billy Pilgrim and Eliot Rosewater go mad; Kilgore Trout secludes himself; and Wilbur Daffodil-11 Swain resorts to drugs. If their collective discovery of the human is imperiling, it is also necessary. It provides the basis for a covenant relation between person and person for mutual validation at a time when conditions have made untenable any other recognition of our human purpose.

The image of the human mind strained by ideological oppression, within a body racked by pain, dominates Vonnegut's novels from the first, without any implication that life ever was or will be less burdened by suffering or exempt from death. But there is a change in Vonnegut's attitude toward his persistently apocalyptic stories, and it comes about through the same psychological introspection which attends his technical development. As the novels penetrate humanity's betrayed trusts in utopian perfectability, economic progress, scientific inquiry, social prerogative, military power, and the innate illusion of personal immortality, Vonnegut gradually affirms a true source of life: consciousness. Consciousness brings him to reject any false foundation for being, or "junk," as he calls it. Trusting in a transcendent source of being frees the human mind from laying its unlived life on institutions, which cannot fulfill the heart's yearning to live. It is significant that where Vonnegut's memory is most highly charged with social injustice and political tragedy, namely, in *Slaughterhouse-Five, Breakfast of Champions,* and *Slapstick,* consciousness holds in check the immense force of doom. Consciousness formulates hope, which is why Vonnegut calls it "sacred." Hope defies explanation, in Vonnegut's reflection, because it lies in the sovereignty of the Creator of the Universe, however unpredictably his will presents itself, and in the sovereignty of human love, however rare its presence. From the dramatic action of the novels, however, we see that Vonnegut addresses that hope to the disenfranchised, who do not nourish the illusion that they are masters of their present or future. This, the message of self-giving love, is the proclamation of Vonnegut's novels. It is the best of all possible news.

I began this book by saying that Vonnegut's writing is like a web unified by the unfolding of his moral thought. One issue that the hero raises in the first novel suggests a way of seeing at what point the evolution of Vonnegut's response to his disintegrating world now stands. Surveying a culture depleted of its humanizing institutions, Paul Proteus bitterly asks, "'And what does an anthropologist do these days?'" In the context of *Player Piano,* the question is rhetorical; but the latest books, *Breakfast of Champions* and *Slapstick,* provide a response from the perspective of many years that one could not have predicted, yet which we can now recognize as gradually emerging from the personal presence Vonnegut has worked toward. The anthropologist and physician can become an artist and write a fictive guide to our lost culture. The result is a new artistic effect.

In *Breakfast of Champions* Vonnegut does not simply survey things gone by; Vonnegut affirms his own identity. His relation to his readers, which he makes a point of establishing, is crucial to his intention here. Through the narrated events, we are to contemplate, to share, to lament, and to learn; and from this knowledge the reader experiences a wholly new feeling of compassion toward the disastrous collisions we have read with our eyes. This increasing awareness is what Vonnegut pictures in the unwavering band of light between him and the reader. For such an encounter the actual tale counts for little, and chronology counts still less. What strikes us is the narrator, Vonnegut himself, as his sensibility grows upon the reader, as he chronicles his responses. Vonnegut's personality seems to transpire through the text. His personality, asserted boldly in the Prologue, then only surmised through tone as Dwayne and Trout follow their collision course, in the end comes through in deeply human terms. The concluding sketch of himself weeping portrays the culminating achievement of his strongest art—a graphic disclosure of Vonnegut's consciousness. His impatience with realistic detail, his indifference to linear story line, and his parodic, almost cartoon, characterizations are negative expressions of his affirmative idea of fiction as a living process of progressive relation to an involved, evolving reader. If fiction gives form to life, its form in turn gives life to us. For Vonnegut, we need fiction to live.

CHRONOLOGY

1922   November 11: Kurt Vonnegut, Jr., is born in Indianapolis, Indiana, to Kurt Vonnegut and Edith Lieber Vonnegut.

1940   Graduates from Shortridge High School, Indianapolis.

1940   Enters Cornell University to study biochemistry.

1941   Spring: begins writing for the *Cornell Sun.*

1941   December 7: the Japanese attack the U. S. naval base at Pearl Harbor.

1942   Spring: becomes managing editor of the *Cornell Sun.*

1942   Fall: transfers to Carnegie Tech in his junior year.

1942   Enters the U. S. Army as an infantry private.

1945   February 13: R. A. F. leads an Allied fire-bombing of Dresden, Germany, where Vonnegut is working as a prisoner of war; 135,000 people are killed.

1945   March 9: the U. S. bombards Tokyo with incendiary and high explosive bombs; 83,793 are killed.

1945   Vonnegut returns home from war decorated with a Purple Heart.

1945   August 6: America makes the first military use of the atomic bomb in the attack on Hiroshima; 71,379 people are killed.

1945   September 1: marries Jane Marie Cox.

1945-47   Studies anthropology at the University of Chicago.

1946   Works as a reporter at the Chicago City News Bureau.

1947-50   Lives in Schenectady, New York, where he works as a public relations writer for the General Electric Research Laboratory.

1950   Leaves his job at General Electric and takes up residence in Barnstable on Cape Cod to devote himself to writing fiction.

1952   Publishes *Player Piano,* his first novel.

1959   Publishes *The Sirens of Titan.*

1961   Publishes *Mother Night.*

1961   Publishes *Canary in a Cat House,* his first collection of short stories.

1963	Publishes *Cat's Cradle.*
1963	November 22: President John Kennedy is assassinated in Dallas.
1965–67	Teaches in the Writers Workshop at the University of Iowa.
1965	Publishes *God Bless You, Mr. Rosewater.*
1965	Begins reviewing for the *New York Times Book Review.*
1967–68	Receives a Guggenheim fellowship.
1968	Publishes *Welcome to the Monkey House,* his second volume of short stories.
1968	March 16: American soldiers sweep through the hamlet of My Lai in Vietnam and gun down at least 109 men, women, and children.
1968	April 4: the Reverend Martin Luther King, Jr., is assassinated in Memphis, Tennessee.
1968	June 5: Senator Robert Kennedy is assassinated in the Hotel Ambassador in Los Angeles.
1969	Vonnegut participates in a symposium on the novel at Brown University.
1969	Publishes *Slaughterhouse-Five.*
1970	January 3: goes to Biafra to assist with shipments of food for the starving African kingdom, which collapses about a week after he departs for home.
1970	Spring: addresses the graduating class of Bennington College.
1970	May 4: four young people are killed by the National Guard in an antiwar protest at Kent State University.
1970	Receives literature award from the National Institute of Arts and Letters.
1970	Fall: teaches writing at Harvard.
1970	October 7: *Happy Birthday, Wanda June,* his play, opens in New York City and runs through March 14, 1971.
1971	Receives his M. A. in anthropology from the University of Chicago.
1972	March 13: *Between Time and Timbuktu,* a ninety-minute special excerpting his fiction, appears on public television.
1973	Publishes *Breakfast of Champions.*
1973	Fall: teaches creative writing at City College of the City University of New York and resigns in February, 1974.
1974	August 8: Richard M. Nixon resigns as President of the United States.
1974	Publishes *Wampeters, Foma & Granfalloons,* a collection of reviews, addresses, and interviews, 1965 to 1973.
1976	Publishes *Slapstick.*
	Vonnegut presently lives in Manhattan.

NOTES

INTRODUCTION

1. *Wampeters, Foma & Granfalloons* (New York: Delacorte Press/ Seymour Lawrence, 1974), p. 285.
2. From an interview with John Casey and Joe David Bellamy in *The New Fiction: Interviews with Innovative American Writers,* ed. by Joe David Bellamy (Urbana: University of Illinois Press, 1974), p. 202.
3. Ibid., p. 205.
4. Ibid.
5. *New York Times Book Review* (March 9, 1975): 2.
6. *Straw for the Fire: From the Notebooks of Theodore Roethke, 1943-1963,* selected and arranged by David Wagoner (Garden City: Anchor Press/Doubleday, 1974), p. 235.
7. *"Playboy* Interview," in *Wampeters, Foma & Granfalloons,* p. 256.
8. "Address to the Graduating Class at Bennington College, 1970," in *Wampeters, Foma & Granfalloons,* p. 163.

CHAPTER ONE

1. Norbert Wiener, *The Human Use of Human Beings: Cybernetics and Society* (New York: Avon Books, 1967), pp. 250-51.
2. James Mooney, *The Ghost Dance,* shortened version edited by A. F. C. Wallace (Chicago: University of Chicago Press, 1965).
3. Weston La Barre, *The Ghost Dance: The Origins of Religion* (New York: Delta Books, 1972), pp. 227-77.

CHAPTER TWO

1. James Mellard, "The Modes of Vonnegut's Fiction: Or, *Player Piano* Ousts *Mechanical Bride* and *The Sirens of Titan* Invade *The Gutenberg*

Galaxy," *The Vonnegut Statement,* ed. Jerome Klinkowitz and John Somer (New York: Dell Publishing Co., 1973), p. 201.

2. Ibid., p. 194.

3. See Northrop Frye, *Anatomy of Criticism* (New York: Atheneum, 1967), pp. 37-38 and 103-04.

4. Karen and Charles Wood, "The Vonnegut Effect: Science Fiction and Beyond," *The Vonnegut Statement,* p. 136.

5. Peter J. Reed, *Kurt Vonnegut, Jr.* (New York: Warner Paperback Library, 1972), p. 58.

6. Jerome Klinkowitz, "Kurt Vonnegut, Jr.: The Canary in a Cathouse," *The Vonnegut Statement,* p. 9.

7. Charles Thomas Samuels, "Age of Vonnegut," *New Republic* CLXIV (June 12, 1971): 30-32.

CHAPTER THREE

1. "A Talk with Kurt Vonnegut, Jr.," in *The Vonnegut Statement,* ed. Jerome Klinkowitz and John Somer (New York: Dell Publishing Co., 1973), p. 115.

2. Ibid.

3. Ihab Hassan, *Contemporary American Literature, 1945-1973* (New York: Frederick Ungar Publishing Co., 1973), p. 46.

4. Jerome Klinkowitz, "The Literary Career of Kurt Vonnegut, Jr.," *Modern Fiction Studies* 19 (Spring, 1973): 59.

5. Tony Tanner, *City of Words: American Fiction 1950-1970* (New York: Harper & Row, 1971), p. 188.

6. See Marjorie Hope Nicolson's splendid study, "The Professor and The Detective," in *The Art of the Mystery Story,* ed. by Howard Haycroft (New York: Simon and Schuster, 1947), pp. 110-27.

CHAPTER FOUR

1. Peter J. Reed, *Kurt Vonnegut, Jr.* (New York: Warner Paperback Library, 1972), p. 119.

2. Max Schulz, *Black Humor Fiction of the Sixties* (Athens: Ohio University Press, 1973), p. 56.

3. David Goldsmith, *Kurt Vonnegut: Fantasist of Fire and Ice* (Bowling Green, Ohio: Bowling Green University Popular Press, 1972), p. 16.

4. Raymond M. Olderman in *Beyond the Waste Land: A Study of the American Novel in the Nineteen-Sixties* (New Haven: Yale University Press, 1972) says that Vonnegut's ideas of the universe are Swiftian but that his response is different (see p. 192). Olderman is correct about their thematic affinities. He does not, however, take up the question of formal parallels.

5. Tony Tanner, *City of Words: American Fiction 1950-1970* (New York: Harper & Row, 1971), p. 191.

6. The observation recurs in Swift criticism. For a particularly intelligent discussion of the issue see Martin Price's *Swift's Rhetorical Art: A Study in Structure and Meaning* (New Haven: Yale University Studies in English, vol. 123, 1953).

7. Northrop Frye, *Fearful Symmetry: A Study of William Blake* (Princeton: Princeton University Press, 1947), p. 198.

8. Harold Bloom, *Blake's Apocalypse* (Ithaca: Cornell University Press, 1963), p. 95.

9. Frye, op. cit., p. 200.

CHAPTER SIX

1. Rudolf Bultmann and Karl Kundsin, *Form Criticism: Two Essays on New Testament Research* (New York: Harper & Row, 1962), p. 160.

2. Paul Tillich, *The New Being* (New York: Charles Scribner's Sons, 1955), p. 103.

3. See Frank Kermode, *The Sense of an Ending: Studies in the Theory of Fiction* (New York: Oxford University Press, 1967).

4. D. H. Lawrence, *Apocalypse,* with an Introduction by Richard Aldington (New York: The Viking Press, 1960), pp. 144-45.

5. Rudolf Bultmann, *Jesus Christ and Mythology* (New York: Charles Scribner's Sons, 1958), p. 68.

6. See Jerome Klinkowitz in *The Vonnegut Statement,* ed. Jerome Klinkowitz and John Somer (New York: Dell Publishing Co., 1973), p. 14.

7. See Loretta McCabe, "An Exclusive Interview with Kurt Vonnegut, Jr.," *Writers Yearbook–1970,* p. 105.

CHAPTER SEVEN

1. Bruce Cook, "When Kurt Vonnegut Talks—And He Does—The Young All Tune In," *National Observer* (October 12, 1970): 21.

2. "*Playboy* Interview" in *Wampeters, Foma & Granfalloons* (New York: Delacorte Press/Seymour Lawrence, 1974), p. 282.

BIBLIOGRAPHY

WORKS BY KURT VONNEGUT, JR.

Player Piano. New York: Charles Scribner's Sons, 1952.
The Sirens of Titan. New York: Dell, 1959.
Mother Night. New York: Fawcett, 1961; reissued with an Introduction, by Harper & Row, 1966.
Canary in a Cat House. New York: Fawcett, 1961.
Cat's Cradle. New York: Holt, Rinehart and Winston, 1963.
God Bless You, Mr. Rosewater. New York: Holt, Rinehart and Winston, 1965.
Welcome to the Monkey House: A Collection of Short Works. New York: Delacorte/Seymour Lawrence, 1968.
Slaughterhouse-Five. New York: Delacorte/Seymour Lawrence, 1969.
Happy Birthday, Wanda June. New York: Delacorte/Seymour Lawrence, 1971.
Between Time and Timbuktu, or Prometheus-5: A Space Fantasy. New York: Delacorte/Seymour Lawrence, 1972.
Breakfast of Champions. New York: Delacorte/Seymour Lawrence, 1973.
Wampeters, Foma & Granfalloons. New York: Delacorte/Seymour Lawrence, 1974.
"Tom Wicker Signifying." Review of *A Time to Die* by Tom Wicker, *New York Times Book Review,* March 9, 1975, pp. 2-3.
Slapstick: or Lonesome No More!. New York: Delacorte/Seymour Lawrence, 1976.

A detailed account of Vonnegut's publications through 1972 is given in *The Vonnegut Statement* edited by Jerome Klinkowitz and John Somer (New York: Dell Publishing Co., 1973).

WORKS ABOUT VONNEGUT AND WORKS CITED

Bellamy, Joe David, ed. *The New Fiction: Interviews with Innovative American Writers.* Urbana: University of Illinois Press, 1974.

Blake, William. *The Poetical Works of William Blake.* London: Oxford University Press, 1961.

Bloom, Harold. *Blake's Apocalypse.* Ithaca: Cornell University Press, 1963.

Bosworth, Patricia. "To Vonnegut, the Hero Is the Man Who Refuses to Kill." *The New York Times,* October 25, 1970, sec. 2, p. 5.

Bryan, C. D. B. "Kurt Vonnegut, Head Bokononist." *The New York Times Book Review,* April 6, 1969, pp. 2, 25.

–––. "Kurt Vonnegut on Target." *New Republic,* October 8, 1966, pp. 21-22, 26.

Bultmann, Rudolf. *Jesus Christ and Mythology.* New York: Charles Scribner's Sons, 1958.

––– and Karl Kundsin. *Form Criticism: Two Essays on New Testament Research.* New York: Harper & Row, 1962.

Cook, Bruce. "When Kurt Vonnegut Talks–And He Does–The Young All Tune In." *National Observer,* October 12, 1970, p. 21.

DeMott, Benjamin. "Vonnegut's Otherworldly Laughter." *Saturday Review,* May 1, 1971, pp. 29-32.

Fiedler, Leslie A. "The Divine Stupidity of Kurt Vonnegut." *Esquire,* September, 1970, pp. 195-204.

Friedman, Bruce Jay, ed. *Black Humor.* New York: Bantam Books, 1965.

Frye, Northrop. *Anatomy of Criticism.* New York: Atheneum, 1967.

–––. *Fearful Symmetry: A Study of William Blake.* Princeton: Princeton University Press, 1947.

Goldsmith, David. *Kurt Vonnegut: Fantasist of Fire and Ice* (Popular Writer Series No. 2). Bowling Green, Ohio: Bowling Green University Popular Press, 1972.

Hassan, Ihab. *Contemporary American Literature, 1945-1973.* New York: Frederick Ungar Publishing Co., 1973.

Hauck, Richard Boyd. *A Cheerful Nihilism: Confidence and "The Absurd" in American Humorous Fiction.* Bloomington: Indiana University Press, 1971.

Henkle, Roger. "Wrestling (American Style) with Proteus." *Novel: A Forum on Fiction* III (Spring 1970): 197-207.

Klinkowitz, Jerome. "Kurt Vonnegut, Jr. and the Crime of His Times." *Critique: Studies in Modern Fiction* XII, no. 3 (1971): 38-53.

–––. "The Literary Career of Kurt Vonnegut, Jr." *Modern Fiction Studies* 19, no. 1 (Spring 1973): 57-67.

––– and John Somer, eds. *The Vonnegut Statement.* New York: Dell Publishing Co., 1973.

La Barre, Weston. *The Ghost Dance: The Origins of Religion.* New York: Delta Books, 1972.

Lawrence, D. H. *Apocalypse,* with an Introduction by Richard Aldington. New York: The Viking Press, 1960.

Leff, Leonard J. "Utopia Reconstructed: Alienation in Vonnegut's *God Bless You, Mr. Rosewater.*" *Critique: Studies in Modern Fiction* XII, no. 3 (1971): 29-37.

McCabe, Loretta. "An Exclusive Interview with Kurt Vonnegut." *Writers Yearbook—1970.* pp. 92-95, 100-01, 103-05.

Mooney, James. *The Ghost Dance,* shortened version edited by A. F. C. Wallace. Chicago: University of Chicago Press, 1965.

Nicolson, Marjorie Hope. "The Professor and The Detective" in Howard Haycroft, ed. *The Art of the Mystery Story.* New York: Simon and Schuster, 1947.

Olderman, Raymond M. *Beyond the Waste Land: A Study of the American Novel in the Nineteen Sixties.* New Haven: Yale University Press, 1972.

Price, Martin. *Swift's Rhetorical Art: A Study in Structure and Meaning.* New Haven: Yale University Press, 1953.

Reed, Peter J. *Kurt Vonnegut, Jr.* New York: Warner Paperback Library, 1972.

Roethke, Theodore. *Straw for the Fire: From the Notebooks of Theodore Roethke, 1943-1963,* selected and arranged by David Wagoner. Garden City: Anchor Press/Doubleday, 1974.

Samuels, Charles Thomas. "Age of Vonnegut." *New Republic* CLXIV (June 12, 1971): 30-32.

Scholes, Robert. *The Fabulators.* New York: Oxford University Press, 1967.

Schulz, Max F. *Black Humor Fiction of the Sixties.* Athens: Ohio University Press, 1973.

———. "The Unconfirmed Thesis: Kurt Vonnegut, Black Humor, and Contemporary Art." *Critique: Studies in Modern Fiction* XII, no. 3 (1971): 5-28.

Swift, Jonathan. *The Writings of Jonathan Swift,* eds. Robert J. Greenberg and William B. Piper. New York: W. W. Norton & Co., 1973.

Tanner, Tony. *City of Words: American Fiction 1950-1970.* New York: Harper & Row, 1971.

Tillich, Paul. *The New Being.* New York: Charles Scribner's Sons, 1955.

Wiener, Norbert. *The Human Use of Human Beings: Cybernetics and Society.* New York: Avon Books, 1967.

INDEX